and

LOTUS

Celtic Christian Spirituality
in the Light of Eastern Wisdom

Vestal, New York 13850

www.AnamcharaBooks.com

paperback ISBN: 978-1-62524-875-6

eBook ISBN: 978-1-62524-876-3

Cover by Ellyn Sanna.
Illustration and layout by Micaela Grace.

OAK
and
LOTUS

Celtic Christian Spirituality
in the Light of Eastern Wisdom

KENNETH MCINTOSH

CONTENTS

1

STRENGTH OF OAK, BEAUTY OF LOTUS

The Fullness of Life

The universe is full of magical things,
patiently waiting for our wits to grow sharper.

—Eden Phillpotts [1]

IN JUNE OF 2020, while millions of people struggled with lockdowns and deprivation caused by the global COVID-19 pandemic, life on Holy Isle in the Firth of Clyde off the west coast of Scotland continued much as it had for the past fifteen hundred years. As one resident said at the time, "I wouldn't say life hasn't changed, but maybe we're among the luckiest people in the UK. We're just getting on with our usual jobs." Islanders farmed salad greens, kale, and potatoes. Wild ponies, goats, and sheep roamed the island as did their ancestors. The human inhabitants of Holy Isle followed a daily pattern of prayers, chants, and meditations—a spiritual intentionality that would have been understood by the sixth-century Celtic monks on the island who emulated their founder Saint Molaise.[2] Then and now, Holy Isle is—as its name implies—a *thin place*. (Theologian and author Bruce Epperly explains thin places as being "present in all things, [but] God can choose to be more present in some places and persons than others. Such places are truly gateways to heaven."[3])

But there is one notable difference between Holy Isle of the past and Holy Isle today. Saint Molaise's hermit cave is still a site of veneration and contemplation, but the rocky overhang is now bedecked with colorful Buddhist prayer flags. And the islands' residents today are Buddhist monks and retreatants learning the ways of the Kagyu school of Tibetan Buddhism.

How did Holy Isle change from a Celtic Christian monastic center to a Mahayana Buddhist one? According to an article in *The Scotsman*, "The island was sold to the Buddhists in 1992 by Kay Morris, a devout Catholic who claimed to have been visited in a dream by the

Virgin Mary, who instructed her to give [the Buddhists] ownership of Holy Isle."[4] The idea of the Virgin Mary smiling on Buddhist monks may seem strange to those accustomed to religious exclusivity, yet the end result of this transfer of the island property has been a growing sense of mutual respect between those who honor Saint Molaise and those who follow the Buddha.[5]

Many twenty-first-century Christ-followers have enriched their faith by rediscovering the ways of ancient Celtic saints and scholars—but what might Christians who follow the Celtic traditions learn from the spiritual practices of Hinduism, Buddhism, or Taoism? This book aims to shed new light on the Celtic Christian pathway from the lanterns of Asian wisdom. I am not proposing some new sort of hybrid religion, a mash-up of ancient traditions, nor am I claiming to be an expert in Eastern religions. Instead, I write to share with you what I have *personally* experienced: *insights from the wisdom of the East have made me a better follower of Christ.*

Several decades ago, I came to a point in my journey where a broader understanding of God and spirituality practically saved my life. I was emotionally shattered; illnesses and crises, compounded by my own poor choices, threatened to tear my life apart. I was a

Christian minister and had faith in God, but my beliefs at that point were inadequate for what I faced.

A therapist suggested I read Anthony De Mello's *The Way to Love*,[6] written by a priest whose life was revolutionized by the spiritual insights he received while in India. From that book, I learned to recognize the power of false attachments. Since adolescence, I'd been basing my happiness on external factors, as well as the need to be in control, to appear all-competent and successful. Now, these attachments were failing me. De Mello's book gave practical instructions on freeing myself from the unhappiness of these entrapments. Progress was gradual and difficult, but I began to feel better, emotionally and spiritually. I like to say that the wisdom of the East "made me born again, again." Years later, I still do some silly things, and I feel afraid at times, but the insights I gained through reading *The Way to Love* definitely set me on a healthier path.

At around that same time, as I was nearing midlife, Celtic Christian spirituality also began to satisfy my thirst for the sacred. As a young man, I had learned about my Scots heritage and the mythology that went along with it, and at age eighteen, I had a profound experience of new birth in Christ—a deflection point that has defined my life ever since. Still, for years I struggled with aspects of Christianity that didn't fit with the truths my heart told me. Some wise guides showed me how the insights of my Gaelic ancestors could soften the stark angles of Christian understanding. I will never say, "This Celtic way is the *one right* way to practice religion" (that would go against the playful and inclusive spirit of this lovely way of being), but it works well for me.

Later on in life, for over a decade, I taught a college course on comparative religions. I sought out teachers from the world's great traditions and had deep discussions with them and my students, striving to enter into others' spiritual adventures. These conversations revealed many connections between all of us who seek understanding and enlightenment, regardless of our particular religious traditions.

This book seeks to synthesize those conversations, along with years of research and travel, into something I can offer to you, the reader. As I began to envision this book, I immediately saw in my mind's eye the oak and the lotus as symbols of Celtic and Eastern wisdom traditions. My life is fuller and richer with the strength of both the oak (Celtic spirituality) and the lotus (Eastern wisdom). I resonate with a friend who says, "Christ is my heart guru." And I understand my Christian faith better in the light of both Asian and Celtic understanding.

The Celtic Oak

The Celts regarded the oak as king of the forest, and still today, the tree serves as a potent symbol for the wisdom of Celtic spirituality. The Celts believed that the tall, strong, and long-living oak trees imparted wisdom, healing, and protection. The oak tree, with its roots deep in the earth and its branches high in the sky, was thought to link the three realms of reality: the Underworld, the "middle earth" in which we live, and Heaven.

The ancient Sanskrit word *duir* is the etymological source for both *oak* and *door,* suggesting that the oak is a portal into greater wisdom, perhaps an entryway into the otherworld itself. Gaelic scholars and spiritual leaders throughout Europe were called *druids* after their word for the oak tree, and to be a druid meant to be "oak wise." Saint Brigid—who shares with Patrick the patronage of Ireland—founded her monastery at the druids' sacred site of Kildare ("place of the oak"). Saint Columba proclaimed, "Christ is my druid," and founded churches in an oak grove at Derry (which means "oak wood"), a monastery at Durrow ("the plain of the oaks"), and yet another monastery at Kells, where Columba lived under an oak tree.

What does it mean to be "oak-wise" today? Anamchara Books' Facebook group lists these eight defining characteristics of Celtic spirituality:

1. *Hope:* We must look for the good rather than the evil in all things.

2. *Environmental stewardship:* The Earth is holy, and we have a Divine call to care for the creatures with whom we share our planet.

3. *Holism:* We must be aware of the sacred in all times and places and refuse to compartmentalize life.

4. *Divine immanence:* God is present in the world, in Nature, in human society, and in all of life.

5. *Love of the arts:* Words, shapes, movement, and music form connections between humans and the Divine.

6. *Mystery:* The world is full of wonder and things beyond our comprehension. The Otherworld is just next door.

7. *Hospitality:* Welcome the stranger, no matter who they are or what they look like.

8. *Equality:* All are equal, deserving of the same respect and care.

The Eastern Lotus

Just as the oak is a potent symbol for Celtic spirituality, the lotus is also a compelling metaphor in Buddhism and other Asian wisdom traditions. It represents the beauty of a life that can transcend anxieties, as well as spiritual enlightenment. *Lion's Roar* magazine says of the lotus plant: "It is rooted in mud (attachment and desire) but its flowers blossom on long stalks unsullied by the mud

below."[7] Like the oak tree, it too links three dimensions: earth, water, and air.

When the Buddha was asked if he was a god, he replied, "Just like a . . . lotus—born in the water, grown in the water, rising up above the water—stands unsmeared by the water, in the same way I—born in the world, grown in the world, having overcome the world—live unsmeared by the world. Remember me, as 'awakened.'"[8] According to legend, wherever the Buddha stepped, a lotus flower bloomed. Countless Buddhist and Hindu paintings, weavings, and statues portray the Buddha or other spiritual figures seated on lotus blossoms.

Interspirituality: An Invitation to Richer Insight

When I taught comparative religions, one of my students was Diné (a member of the Navajo Nation). His family had recently converted to Christianity, and he loved Jesus. At the same time, he felt that many of the traditional Diné spiritual ways were an inseparable part of him. He was conflicted—what could he do to resolve his two spiritual paths? Then, during one class session, we watched a movie about the life of Saint Patrick that explained how Patrick brought the Christ-faith to Ireland while at the same time respecting indigenous Irish traditions. The student was inspired by

OAK AND LOTUS

this portrayal of Ireland's saint, and Patrick's example helped him navigate his own interspiritual path. He realized that his commitment to follow Jesus did not mean he had to abandon his Diné spiritual beliefs.

When Christians, Hindus, Buddhists, and Taoists share spiritual insights with one another—not just to learn facts nor to try to convert one another but rather to benefit from each other's wisdom—they engage in what Brother Wayne Teasdale, a Catholic monastic, calls *interspirituality*.[9] My spiritual mentor identifies as a "Zen Baptist," and a family member identifies as "Budeo-Christian"; they are both expressing the value of inter-spirituality in their lives. As the Dalai Lama explains, "Honor another's religion, for doing so strengthens both one's own and that of the other."[10] Or as Christian spiri-tual director John R. Mabry puts it, "I get closer to Jesus, using the Buddha as a lens."[11]

Some of the most brilliant spiritual minds of mod-ern times were pioneer interspiritual explorers whose witness beckons us onto the same life-giving path. Mahatma Gandhi spoke often of his admiration for the teachings of Jesus, saying, "The New Testament gave me comfort and boundless joy."[12] In turn, Gandhi's life and teachings inspired Martin Luther King, Jr. in his struggle against racism. King said in a sermon, "Christ showed us the way and Gandhi in India showed it could work."[13] Likewise, Trappist monk Thomas Merton told a colleague shortly before he died, "I do not believe that I could understand our Christian faith the way I understand it if it were not for the light of Buddhism."[14]

Have you ever noticed how a gifted photographer can take a familiar subject—a landscape, or person, or object—and by application of the camera's angle or lens filter enable you to see that subject in a completely new way, like you are beholding it for the first time? In the same way, viewing familiar ideas and practices of your faith through the unfamiliar "lens" of another person's spirituality can allow you to see new beauty in familiar faith. It can also open up entirely new insights into your faith. As Richard Rohr says in his book *The Universal Christ*, "I am convinced that in many ways Buddhism and Christianity . . . reveal each other's blind spots."[15]

To be clear, I am not saying by any means that Buddhism is really just a version of Christianity, or that Hinduism and Christianity can be mashed up together into a single belief system. While all religions share some degree of common ground, at the same time each is unique. All reality is unitive (a fact attested to by quantum physics, as well as the perennial notions of Spirit), and at the same time, all reality is particular. Even identical twins differ subtly, as each physical manifestation of the One is unique. So when speaking with followers of differing spiritual traditions, we can affirm both the *oneness* and also the *uniqueness* of our diverse ways—and it is important that we do both.

I also want to be clear that all religious traditions contain within them many variations. An Evangelical Christian and an Orthodox monk will have many differences in beliefs, and so too do the followers of Buddhism's, Hinduism's, and Taoism's many branches. Every religion has some groups who define their faith by theological doctrines and outward forms, while other groups value unmediated experiences of the Divine over concrete words or forms of observance. As spiritual teacher Eknath Easwaran observed, "Theologians may quarrel, but the mystics of the world speak the same language."[16] The scope of this book, as well as my own ignorance, prevents me from discussing in thorough detail the varieties of Eastern religions. Instead, this book prioritizes the mystic heart of each tradition.

I believe humanity's diverse cultures all contain their own unique expressions of their encounters with God, each appropriate to their circumstances in time and place. This means the indigenous beliefs of

Maoris, Meccans, and Mohawks all express Divine truth. It means that before they had any awareness of Christianity, people in Australia, Siberia, and Rapa Nui had already encountered the Divinity. God scattered truth concerning the Divine Self throughout the entire species of humanity.

The apostle Paul, in a sermon he preached in the Aeropagus, the open-air intellectual marketplace of classical Athens, said: "In God we live and move and have our being" (Acts 17). With this statement, Paul establishes the Christian doctrine of panentheism, which states that all things (*pan*) exist within (*en*) the greater reality that is God (*theos*). Panentheism is also integral to the perennial wisdom found in Asia, and many Jews and Christians have shared that belief. In setting forth this essential piece of spiritual doctrine, Paul directly quoted the pre-Christian Greek scholar Epimenides. Clearly, the apostle Paul—who wrote large portions of the Christian scripture—knew and affirmed the value of exchange between differing spiritual traditions. As the nineteenth-century Hindu mystic Sri Ramakrishna reminded, we may have different beliefs, "but all doctrines are only so many paths—and a path is by no means God," only a route to God.

Weaving the Knotwork of Faith Traditions

For the ancient Gaelic peoples, truth and knowledge from many different spheres were interwoven in the Divine knotwork of reality. Legends of the Celtic saints reveal an openness to truths beyond the Bible and Church tradition. Those of us who follow in the contemporary Celtic spiritual way can likewise benefit from a spirit of openness.

While some myths allege that Patrick drove the serpents—a metaphor for paganism—out of Ireland, other myths tell of his honoring the wisdom that was in Ireland before he was. The story "Patrick and the Big Men from Out of the Past" affirms the value of preserving pre-Christian wisdom. The legend relates how "great men from another time"[17] approach Saint Patrick while he is celebrating the Eucharist with his disciples. When Patrick inquires how these men survived for such a long time, their leader, Caoilte, replies, "Truth was in our hearts, and strength in our hands, and fulfillment in our tongues." While the group is talking, two angels come, and Patrick asks them "if it was any harm before the King of Heaven and earth" to listen to these Pagan men. The angels then instruct the patron saint of Ireland: "Whatever they tell, write it down on poets' boards and in the words of poets, for it will be well for the people of the latter times to be listening to them."[18]

Evidence of the Celtic saints' broad interest in all sorts of knowledge—wisdom that extended from beyond orthodox Christian sources—is proven most tangibly in the wealth of diverse texts they copied and preserved for future generations. Popular historian Thomas Cahill in his book *How the Irish Saved Civilization* affirmed that "Irish generosity extended not only to a variety of people but to a variety of ideas . . . they brought into their libraries everything they could lay their hands on. They were resolved to shut out nothing."[19] Meanwhile, their Christian contemporaries in other lands were suspicious of any knowledge that did not come explicitly from scripture or Church writers; the great Bible translator Jerome, for example, feared he might burn in hell for reading Cicero.[20] The Irish scribes, however, "began to devour all of the old Greek and Latin pagan literature that came their way."[21]

While there is no evidence of the Celtic saints meeting Hindu gurus or reading the works of Buddhist monks, I have little doubt that had the Celts had these opportunities, they would have asked many questions and carefully written down all they learned. This book is a modest attempt—centuries later—to create such a discussion between the wisdom of the Celtic West and that of Asia.

Consider this book as a set of trailheads along a roadway. Some ideas may draw you into new adventures, while others you may glance at and pass by. I am not providing you with a detailed map of the paths that lead from each trailhead; if you chose to make this journey for yourself, you will discover your own adventures and insights. I am merely showing you some of the openings into those trails.

The following chapters will compare elements of Celtic Christianity with Hinduism, Buddhism, and Taoism, respectively. Each chapter includes questions, either for private introspection or for group study, as well as practices for exploration and transformation.

DISCUSSION QUESTIONS

What are your thoughts about interspirituality? Are you excited—or apprehensive?

What has been your personal experience with other faiths?

What has been your personal experience of Celtic spirituality?

Can you think of a time when an insight from a faith tradition outside your own helped you to understand your own spiritual path in a deeper way?

SPIRITUAL PRACTICE

A practice that's central to Celtic spirituality but is also appropriate from a Buddhist perspective is the *caim* (circle) prayer. For the ancient Celts, the circle was the primary and most powerful geometric form. The sun—the source of all life on Earth and a symbol of Christ—was a circle, as was the sun's paler partner, the moon, which ruled over feminine energies. The rounded form of a woman's belly spoke of the curving power of new life. Celtic forts, animal pens, and homes were round. (Archaeologists can distinguish ancient Celtic settlements from those of neighboring cultures because Celtic houses were round rather than square or oval).[22] Circles signified life, protection, family, clan, and divinity.

Likewise, circles have significant religious meaning in Eastern philosophies. In an article for *Lion's Roar*, John Steven writes, "*Enso*, a Japanese word meaning 'circular form' and usually translated into English as 'Zen circle,' is a symbol of Buddhist enlightenment. Right from the beginning of the Buddhist tradition, enlightenment was compared to the 'bright full moon' and a 'great round mirror.' . . . Bodhidharma, the grand patriarch of Zen, was called the 'Great Teacher of Circle Enlightenment.'"[23]

I do not conceive of *caim* prayer as magic; it is not an invisible forcefield that will shield from illness or misfortune. Instead, I think of it as God hugging the one who prays—the embrace of a perfectly loving Divine Parent. I find power and healing in the circle prayer.

Begin by establishing a circle around yourself or the person or object you wish to encircle. You may spin around, point with your hand, or even draw a line in sand or dirt. You may wish to walk clockwise (sunwise) around the space you are enfolding in prayer.

The basic form of the prayer is:

Circle me, Divine Love.
Keep evil out, keep good within.
Keep fear without, keep hope within.
Keep hatred out, keep peace within.

Now, as you begin on this new path of interspiritual learning, you may wish to encircle your own soul:

Circle this new spiritual journey, O Divine Love.
Circle the space where I study, pray, and learn.

You can also add a fill-in-the-blank portion of prayer, as your heart guides you:

Keep _____ without, keep _____ within.
Keep confusion without, keep clarity within.
Keep dimness without, keep light within (and so on).

The circle prayer is a practice used by many people for a very long time. It combines the mental, visual, and tactile parts of our being. It is a way to co-create reality with the One.

2

CELTIC SPIRITUALITY AND HINDUISM

Seeing God in Everything

I saw Christ today,
hungry
outside my windows in the winter cold,
and I filled my birdfeeders
that He might be filled.
I saw Christ today,
running on swift hooves across the road,
and I slowed my car that He might be safe.
I saw Christ today,
in the glad face of my dog,
and I greeted her at the end of the workday.
I saw Christ today,
in the moth that beat against the window,
until I let it out into the night.

Each time I saw Christ,
He blessed me,
in the Holy Name of the Trinity,
and the bird outside my window sang
again and again,
Often and often, goes Christ
on wing and hoof and paw.

—Ellyn Sanna[24]

Sunlight nudges me awake, and the scent of pine needles fills my nostrils. I'm a bit cold and a whole lot stiff, confined in the bounds of a mummy sleeping bag beneath a tarp strung between trees. A look out the open front of the shelter reveals a breathtaking view.

The day before, I'd ascended the San Francisco Peaks in Northern Arizona to be alone with the mountain, the susurration of pine needles and aspen leaves my only companionship. A 5,000-foot ascent carrying a pack left my knees aching. Throughout the night, a snorting elk kept stomping around the campsite, and—despite a pair of fallen logs that protected me—I kept waking up afraid the beast would trample me.

But this morning made it all worthwhile. Stepping out from beneath the polypropylene enclosure I beheld a sight that made my heart jump: the backside of a familiar mountain range, mile after mile of unbroken pine and aspen forest. Sunrise set the entire vast panorama ablaze with golden beams that swept across the landscape in a visibly advancing realm of light.

For the duration of that sunrise, I was bursting with joy. This is what it was like to be alive—more truly alive than during the bulk of my ordinary days. I realized that this is how God sees the world each morning: as a dazzling beloved. While I felt love for God, at the same time the love of God for the world warmed me. It was a moment of singular delight and awareness.

I'm not the only person who has had moments of illumination when the natural world reveals itself to be infused with the Divine. There's a reason why holy people are associated with mountaintops and why we have the expression *mountaintop experience*. Surfers and swimmers often feel the same about the deep, and in the Bible, everyone from Hagar to Jesus had intense encounters with the Divine while alone in the "desert" (a word that referred to wilderness areas).

Bede Griffiths, a Catholic priest whose adult identity was shaped by his interspiritual experiences in India, wrote about a foundational experience he had as a child:

> One day during my last term at school I walked out alone in the evening and heard the birds singing in that full chorus of song. . . . I remember now the shock of surprise with which the sound broke on my ears. It seemed that I had never heard the birds singing before and I wondered whether they sang like this all the year round and never noticed it. As I walked on I came upon some hawthorn trees in full bloom and again I thought that I had never seen such a sight or experienced such sweetness before. If I had been brought suddenly among the trees of the Garden of Paradise and heard a choir of angels singing I could not have been more surprised. I came thus to where the sun was setting over the playing fields. A lark rose suddenly from the ground beside the tree where I was standing and poured out its song above my head, and then sank still singing to rest. Everything then grew still as the sunset faded and the veil of

dusk began to cover the earth. I remember now the feeling of awe which came over me. I felt inclined to kneel on the ground, as though I had been standing in the presence of angel.[25]

Such moments of transcendental clarity need not come only in pristine natural environments. On March 18, 1958, for example, Thomas Merton was doing errands in downtown Louisville when he had a life-changing epiphany. Today a historical marker marks the spot of Merton's revelation on a busy street next to a bike rack, which—when I was there—bears a bit of graffiti, testimony to how the sacred is concealed in the ordinary. It's unique as the only historical marker in the United States that commemorates a mystical experience.

Merton described this experience in *Conjectures of a Guilty Bystander*:

In Louisville, at the corner of Fourth and Walnut, in the center of the shopping district, I was suddenly overwhelmed with the realization that I loved all those people. . . . It was like waking from a dream of separateness. . . . This sense of liberation from an illusory difference was such a relief and such a joy to me that I almost laughed out loud! And if only everybody could realize this! But it cannot be explained. There is no way of telling people that they are all walking around shining like the sun.[26]

Such serendipitous illuminations of love are not unique to Christianity. Since the time when civilization first dawned in the Indus Valley, Vedic sages, who wrote many of Hinduism's sacred scriptures, sought to experience the Divine Reality concealed in ordinary Nature, objects, and events. Their insights, coupled with those of ancient Celtic Christians, offer us today clues to how we can experience God in everything.

Ancient Paths That Intertwine

In my experiences writing and speaking on Celtic spirituality, many people from India have told me, "This Celtic spirituality seems familiar." There could be a good reason for this: a long-standing scholarly theory holds that a group of people left the Eurasian steppes five thousand years ago, some migrating north into Europe, while others from the same group went south into India. As a result, Vedic and Gaelic languages and cultures share common qualities.

Respected Harvard professor of linguistics Calvert Watkins pointed to numerous similarities between Old Irish and Vedic Sanskrit linguistic structure and wording. For example, in Old Irish, *arya* means "freeman," while in Sanskrit, *aire* means "noble"; in Old Irish, *naib* means "good," and in Sanskrit, *noeib* means "holy"; in Old Irish, *badhira* means "deaf," and in Sanskrit, *bodhar* means "deaf'"; *names* means "respect" in Old Irish, and in Sanskrit, the word is *nemed*; *righ* is the Old Irish word for "king," while *raja* is the Sanskrit word.[27] Professor Watkins built an entire career writing about these and countless other similarities between the ancient language.

The ancient Celts and Vedics shared commonalities in their religious mythologies as well. Among the ancient Celts, Danu, for instance, was the "Mother Goddess," the "Divine Waters" that fell from heaven to water the Earth, who gave her name to the River Danube. Meanwhile, in Sanskrit, *danu* also means "Divine waters." Danu appears in the Vedic story "The Churning of the Oceans," a story with parallels in Irish and Welsh mythology.[28]

There are numerous other similarities between Celtic and Vedic culture and religion. Celtic gods and goddesses embodied Nature; taught ethics, justice, knowledge, speech, arts, crafts, and medicine; gave courage during war and battled forces of darkness; and often had multiple other functions. By comparison, the early Vedic pantheon included deities of fire, solar, atmospheric, and other Nature forces; taught speech, crafts, arts, harvests, medicine, justice, and ethical/ecological order; directed humans during war and battled malevolent beings; and, like their Celtic counterparts, often had overlapping functions. Druids memorized lengthy free-form poetic sagas, with a three-part cadence at the end, which communicated spiritual insight and civic laws. Vedic bards also memorized long sagas that conveyed spiritual knowledge and dharmic duty in free form, also with a three-part cadence at the end. Druids practiced breathing, posture, and meditation techniques that promoted spiritual insight and ecstasy, often accompanied by intense heat in the body, while Vedic ascetics practiced breathing, posture, and meditation skills in a spiritual unfoldment process that generated body heat. Celts honored women, guarded their virtue, and allowed daughters of sonless fathers to inherit property; seeresses and priestesses were respected and heeded. Vedics valued women, and by law, sonless fathers could bequeath property to daughters; female seers were honored. The Celtic earth realm was called *bitus*, and Celtic gods were called *deuos*, "shining ones"; the Vedic word for the earth world was *bhu,* and the gods of the Vedas were *deva*, meaning "shining ones." The Celts' priests taught that human souls were indestructible; departed souls dwelled in the Otherworld until their next reincarnation as a human or animal. Meanwhile, according to Vedic writings, souls continue to exist after death in an Otherworld until they enter another human or animal body. The Celtic universe ends and rebuilds through fire and water in a repeating cycle, and the Vedic universe has a repeating creation-destruction cycle through fire and water.[29]

Apparently, both the Celts and the Vedic Hindus believed their gods loved music. Recognizing music's spiritual power of music is almost universal in ancient traditions, of course, but musicologists have found distinct similarities between these two ancient musical traditions. The Irish music critic Fanny Feehan told of a time when she played a recording of an old Irish folk tune for an Indian professor of music; until the Indian professor saw the record sleeve, she refused to believe it was an Irish song, because, she said, it was nearly identical to the melody of an Indian raga. The Irish song begins with the words, "Come with me to the mountain," while the raga tells the story of a young girl being lured toward a mountain.[30] Historian Bryan McMahon plays a game where he hums the first few notes of Irish folk songs and then asks Indians to complete the songs however they like. He says that almost every time, the Indians will sing the remaining notes as if they already know the songs.[31]

Celtic cosmology also paralleled Vedic cosmology. Like the ancient Celtic astrologers who used a system based on twenty-seven lunar mansions, Vedic writings refer to *nakshatras,* the twenty-seven divisions of their star map.[32] King Ailill of Connacht, Ireland, like the Moon in Vedic mythology, was said to have a circular palace with twenty-seven windows through which he could gaze on his twenty-seven "star wives."[33]

Preeminent scholar of Celtic history Peter Berresford Ellis points out many other societal similarities between Celtic and Vedic cultures. Both divided citizens according to their roles in life. The Vedic Brahmins seem much like the early Celtic druids; both were society's intelligentsia, learned in law, medicine, astronomy, and spiritual wisdom.[34]

Another intriguing similarity between ancient Celtic and Vedic mythology relates to cows. As scholar Doris Srinivasan pointed out, in the Vedic scriptures "the cow pouring out a flood of milk" is an analogy for everything from light to the cosmic waters to poetic vision.[35] Vishnu, one of Hinduism's principal deities, is said to recline on an ocean of milk, and in Hinduism, Nature is often thought of as the ocean of milk that supplies all living things with abundant nourishment. The "churning" of this sea of milk produces the changing expressions of life, both physically and spiritually. Bhudevi, the Earth goddess, is visualized as a cow whose milk sustains all life.[36] Similarly, medieval Irish manuscripts refer to many magical milkers, including Glas Ghaibhleann, the Grey Cow of the Smith, who gives enough milk to feed the whole world.[37] The name of one of the most important goddesses of ancient Ireland, Bóand, means "illuminated cow"

(the River Boyne was named in her honor).[38] Cows show up in other Celtic stories, including ones about that most famous of Celtic saints, Brigid. Legend says Brigid's mother was carrying a pitcher of milk when she gave birth, and she used the milk to bathe her newborn daughter. Brigid was reared on the milk of a white, red-eared cow, and as an adult, she had a cow as her companion, who gave her all the milk she required. As the abbess at Kildare, she miraculously increased the milk and butter yield of the abbey. Some stories said her cow produced a lake of milk three times a day and filled hundreds of baskets with butter.[39]

I could continue with these comparisons, but there's a level at which you can perceive the connections between ancient Indian and Celtic cultures more intuitively. Look at the flowing ornate patterns carved into the white stone of Indian temples, watch the exquisite hand and foot gestures of a Bharatanatyam dancer, or listen to the interwoven melodies of sitar, flute, and table. Then recall the extraordinarily detailed knotwork filled with vibrant colors in Celtic manuscripts such as the Book of Kells or Lindisfarne Gospels. Hear the soul-stirring melodies of an Irish musical session with pipe, fiddle, bodhran. Gaze at the sculpted details of a Celtic stone cross. Both Hindu and Celtic artistic forms are intrinsically spiritual, produced by artists and sages who knew mystical realities. Both traditions celebrate the interconnectedness and the goodness underlying the mundane world, hinting at deep common roots from millennia ago.

Clouded Perceptions

When teaching comparative religions in a college setting, I often introduced Hinduism by showing a short video clip from *The Matrix*, the scene where Morpheus holds out his palms to Neo, his right holding a red pill, and a blue pill in his left, saying, "You take the Blue Pill, the story ends. You wake up in your bed and believe whatever you want to believe. You take the Red Pill, you stay in Wonderland and I show you how deep the rabbit hole goes. I'm only offering you the truth, nothing more." When Neo consumes the red pill, he realizes the world is very different from what he has hitherto experienced. What he had always before assumed to be reality is in fact the Matrix, a constantly projected illusion.

This scene is an effective way to introduce students to a basic element of the Eastern wisdom traditions: Hinduism, Buddhism, and Taoism all agree that *to some degree our perceptions of what is real and important are clouded.* Christianity—including its Celtic form—shares this same spiritual premise.

The elusive reality of the world-as-we-perceive-it can be proven by a simple demonstration. Without a doubt, as you read this, you are near a solid object like a desk or a chair (or this book, in print or tablet form)—so now, *try pushing your hands through that object.* You're not even going to try, right? Because you know it's ridiculous. You know a solid object (your body) will not go through another solid object (whether a desk, chair, or book). *But just how solid are our bodies?* They're made entirely of atoms—and a hydrogen atom is about 99.9999999999996 percent empty space.[40] We know from "experience" that we are solid objects—and yet science says we are actually a vast amount of empty space. Reality is more than what we commonly perceive.

For Hindus, our common interpretation of reality is clouded by *Maya.* The meaning of this concept is subtle and easily misunderstood. Although the word is often translated as "illusion," belief in Maya doesn't indicate that the world around us is simply a figment of our imagination. Instead, *Maya* means that the world is not as it seems; the world we experience is misleading, hiding its true nature from our perception. As Nemo discovered in *The Matrix,* an accurate vision of reality is tricky; we should learn to question our perceptions regarding both weal and woe, for things that appear negative may actually contain blessing (and things that appear positive may actually be destructive).

From a dualistic perspective, this ambivalence regarding the reliability of our senses is hard to understand. By *dualism,* I'm referring here to the assumption that consciousness (ideas, thoughts, perceptions) belong to a different realm than matter does, and that the spiritual and the physical exist in separate realities. According to this way of thinking—which is habitual to most of us Westerners—something either *is* or *is not,* but it cannot be both. Our dualistic minds are stuck in either-or thinking. The perennial wisdom of the East challenges this foundational assumption of the Western mind, and instead, Eastern thought uses as its default the idea that reality is *both-and.* This *nondual* way of understanding the world has no difficulty comprehending that matter is *both* solid *and* nearly all empty space. By the same token, according to nondualistic thinking, we do not live in a physical reality we will leave behind when we die and enter spiritual reality; instead, *all* reality is *both* physical *and* spiritual. And on the one hand, the world is Maya: the things that draw our interest, our appetites, and desires may not be as desirable as they seem. On the other hand, the material world is the precious container of the ultimate Good—Divinity who is Pure Love. As quantum physics has discovered, reality is relative to how we perceive it. Our perceptions change its nature.

The Hindu idea of Maya offers us a lens to see similar concepts in Judaism and Christianity. *Olam*, the word used in the Hebrew Bible for "world" or "universe" derives from a root word that means "hidden." As Martin Luther once wrote, "The world is God's mask." Luther believed, however, that visible, tangible reality is not something separate from God, a veil hanging between our senses and the Divine that clouds our perceptions, but rather that God actively participates in reality; it is where, Luther said, Divinity not only hides but also is busy with the ongoing work of creation. God hides in reality so that we may discover God there.[41] Once again, it all depends on our perspective.

In the Hebrew scriptures, in the Book of Ecclesiastes, the writer says again and again that everything is *havel*. This word has often been translated as "emptiness"; wealth, pleasures, learning, power, success, possessions, and experiences—*everything,* says the ancient author, is emptiness. The literal meaning of *havel* is "vapor," something that is fleeting and ephemeral, something that clouds our perceptions of what is truly *real.* The long-ago Jewish sage would have agreed with the rock band Kansas: everything is "dust in the wind."

The Christian scriptures also assert both the goodness and the fallenness of Creation. This non-dual perspective of reality in the Bible is obvious when you see that the same author on the one hand writes, "Do not love the world or anything in the world. . . . For everything in the world . . . passes away" (1 John 2:15–17)—and, then just two chapters later, says, "Love comes from God. Everyone who loves has been born of God and knows God. Whoever does not love does not know God, because God is love. This is how God showed his love among us: He sent his one and only Son into the world that we might live through him" (4:7–9). John understands both *the world* and *love* in a nondual way.

Although modern adherents of Celtic Christianity say over and over that their spirituality affirms the *goodness* of creation, the Celtic Christ-followers of the Early Middle Ages perceived the world as *both* deceptive *and* good. The *Carmina Gadelica*, a Victorian-era collection of ancient Scottish folklore, contains this affirming prayer:

Bless to me, O God,
Each thing mine eye sees;
Bless to me, O God,
Each sound mine ear hears;
Bless to me, O God,
Each odour that goes to my nostrils
Bless to me, O God,
Each taste that goes to my lips;
Each note that goes to my song,
Each ray that guides my way,
Each thing that I pursue.[42]

On the other hand, the sermons of the sixth-century Irish evangelist Columbanus, who brought the Christian Gospel to many rural regions in what we now call Europe often point to the transitory and illusory nature of our lives. In a typical message, Columbanus declares, "Human life, fragile and marked for death, how many have you deceived, beguiled and blinded? While in flight, you are nothing; while in sight, you are but a shadow; while you rise up, you are but smoke."[43] Ancient Celtic saints agreed with Hindu sages: our perceptions are often clouded by delusion.

New Sight

Now for the good news. In Hinduism (and also in the Bible and in the traditions of Celtic spirituality), *freedom from delusion is possible*. Humans can achieve a state of existence in which they experience the inner reality of things and therefore eschew false understandings and values. In Eastern wisdom traditions, this is called "awakening" or "enlightenment." (An understanding of "enlightenment" is actually far more complicated—and also disputed—but for our purposes, this is a good shorthand understanding of the term.)

Enlightenment also has a role in Christian faith and practice. Episcopal priest, author, and mystic Cynthia Bourgeault says, "For the earliest Christians, Jesus was not the Savior but the Life-Giver," and she goes on to explain that "salvation was understood as a bestowal of life, and to be saved was to be 'made alive.' . . . Nowadays," she concludes, we'd call Jesus "'the Enlightened One.' Jesus' followers saw him as a master of consciousness, offering a path through which they, too, could become . . . enlightened ones."[44]

Eastern wisdom traditions remind Christ-followers that spiritual life can bring a shift in perception. Such a shift most often comes in glimpses, or in moments of amazing clarity that help us afterward to see life in a different way. Very different experiences—surviving a car crash, nearly losing a loved one in a medical crisis, surfing a big wave, viewing a sunrise—can shock us out of our mundane state and allow sudden illumination.

I knew a man who went unexpectedly into a coma, during which he had an out-of-body encounter with God. Prior to that, he hadn't been a very likable person; he was often angry and abusive of others—but he awoke from his coma an astonishingly new person. From then on, he was a kind and joyful person. That one dramatic experience left an indelible mark on him, which he understood as being "born again," a term that does seem to describe the lasting impact on his personality and character.

The Hindu concept of enlightenment gives us a lens through which we can see new meaning in that famous evangelical phrase, "born again." Some Christians use the term to describe a transaction that assures our passage through the Pearly Gates, the ultimate "Get out of Jail" card. Biblically, however, it means far more than that. In the third chapter of John's Gospel, when Jesus says, "You must be born again," he wasn't talking about heaven or hell. Instead, Jesus' call to new birth is an invitation to go beyond our clouded perceptions of reality—to open our consciousness so that we see the Divine in all things. Jesus' invitation to new birth can be seen as an opportunity to set our perceptions free from the limitations of *Maya*.

The Celtic Christian tradition also speaks of "seeing beyond." According to ancient tales, a guardian angel named Victor guided Saint Patrick through his life's important decisions.[45] According to *The Life of Columba,* written by someone who knew Columba firsthand, the saint often saw either angels or demons hidden in the guise of ordinary things. George McLeod, the Scottish minister and mystic who refounded Iona Abbey as a place of worship in the twentieth century, said: "Invisible we see you, Christ beneath us. . . . With earthly eyes we see beneath us stones and dust and dross. . . . But with the eye of faith, we know you uphold. In you all things consist and hang together; the very atom is light energy, the grass is vibrant, the rocks pulsate . . . turn but a stone and an angel moves."[46]

What is it that Maya hides from us? What is the missing dimension of our ordinary seeing? Ah, that is Glory! It is the Divine, God in everything, that waits for our seeing.

In an age of burgeoning authoritarianism, racism, hatred, violence, and climate catastrophe, how can a sane person remain joyful? The either-or mind can cause people to catastrophize, to be cast down utterly by the extent of the world's suffering. Nondual thinking, on the other hand, can enable us to live courageously—even joyfully—in a world beset by existential challenges. It offers us a glorious freedom. Yes, the world is broken—*and* it is also permeated with Divine Presence, shot through with God's Splendor. "Earth's crammed with heaven," as poet Elizabeth Barrett Browning wrote, "and every common bush afire with God."

Aɴ All-iɴ-God View oꜰ Realiᴄy

Foreigners have often misunderstood Hinduism. An outside observer might say with Mark Twain, "India has 2,000,000 gods and worships them all."[47] Officially, there are thirty-three different Hindu deities—or, as some Hindus say, 330 million!

If you have even a passing acquaintance with Hinduism, you have likely seen portrayals of Ganesh, the elephant deity who is the beloved Remover of Obstacles. Or Shiva, the cosmic Lord of the Dance, spinning worlds into being with his swirling limbs. Perhaps you are familiar with Kali, blue-skinned and fierce. Over the centuries, various gods and goddesses have fallen and risen in popularity. Today, the different strands of Hinduism and different geographical regions all emphasize different ideas about how the Divine manifests. Each deity is an expression of the Divine Presence that fills all reality.

Because of this vast pantheon, Westerners often assume that all Hindus are polytheistic (having

many gods and goddesses). Yet that is not always so, for many Hindus regard all these exalted beings as *manifestations* of one supreme Being whom they worship by many names.[48] This is expressed poetically in the Shvetashvatara Upanishad:

> *He is fire and the sun,*
> *and the moon and the stars.*
> *He is this boy,*
> *he is that girl,*
> *he is this man,*
> *he is that woman,*
> *and he is this old man too, tottering on his staff.*
> *His face is everywhere.*
> *He is the blue bird;*
> *he is the green bird with red eyes:*
> *he is the thundercloud,*
> *and he is the seasons and the seas.*[49]

An ancient Celtic poem, one of the oldest in existence, expresses similar ideas about the Divine Spirit:

> *I am Wind on Sea,*
> *I am Ocean-wave,*
> *I am Roar of Sea,*
> *I am Bull of Seven Fights,*

I am Vulture on Cliff,
I am Dewdrop,
I am Fairest of Flowers,
I am Boar for Boldness,
I am Salmon in Pool,
I am Lake on Plain,
I am a Mountain and a Man,
I am a Poem, a Word of Skill,
I am the Point of a Weapon,
I am God who fashions Fire in the Human Head,
Who smooths the Ruggedness of a Mountain.[50]

Both Hinduism and Celtic spirituality see the Divine embodied everywhere—in the goddesses and gods, but also in Nature, in animals, and in other human beings.[51] The Katha Upanishad puts it like this:

God is the sun shining in the sky,
The wind blowing in space;
He is the fire at the altar and in the home the guest.
He dwells in human beings, in gods, in truth,
And in the vast firmament;
He is the fish born in water, the
plant growing in the earth,
The river flowing down from the mountain,
For He is supreme.[52]

Incarnation and Avatar

Christians refer to the embodiment of Divinity as *incarnation;* they may not realize the Hindu term *avatar* has a very similar meaning. In the twenty-first century, many of us think of an avatar as a computer-generated icon or figure that represents a user in online games, chatrooms, and other forms of virtual reality—but the Sanskrit meaning of *avatar* is "descent," with the implication of "to alight, to make an appearance,"[53] and in Hinduism, the word refers to the physical appearance—the incarnation—of Deity. According to Hindu scholar Pavulraj Michael, *avatar* "designates the participation of God in the world of human beings to bring righteousness and salvation. . . . [T]he scope of God's descent among human beings is directed towards the restoration of justice." Michael goes on to say that the doctrine of *avatar* teaches us that the Divine is "deeply and intimately a personal God."

- "God becomes incarnate for the purpose of salvation, which consists of eternal communion" with the Divine.

- "God in kindness and grace takes human form" to rescue us. We are saved by seeing God's "essential nature, deeds, and teachings."

- God becomes incarnate "for the supreme goodness of fulfilling the will of God."

"Thus," says Michael, " the *avatar* steps down from the throne of God to reach the human soul struggling . . . to identify with God." Through the avatar, God suffers with human beings, "endures pain with them and leads them by the hand like a friend or comrade or guide." [54] This sounds a lot like the Christian understanding of Divine Incarnation in Jesus!

Traditionally, however, Christians have believed the Incarnation happened only once, in the Person of Jesus, while Hindus, believing that each period of human history has its own unique needs, see the concept of *avatar* as something that happens again and again. The Divine appears to us, according to Hinduism, in many shapes and forms. This is consistent with the Hindu view that time is cyclical and that reality is destroyed and recreated again and again. Meanwhile, the Western world thinks of time as linear, and so God needs to take on flesh only once for the Incarnation to change our world.

The Pagan Celts would have been at home with the Hindu understanding of Divinity, but with the coming of Christianity to Celtic lands, the Celts fell passionately in love with Jesus, the unique, incarnated Child of God and Humanity. Although some early Christ-followers doubted that Jesus had an actual flesh-and-blood body, the Celts joyously affirmed that Jesus was no "vaporous and empty apparition"[55] but a breathing, laughing, eating, sleeping, loving human being like themselves (while still being totally Divine). Celtic Christianity believed God participates in the human world through Christ—and that Christ continues to be incarnated in those who are oppressed and suffering, as well as in ourselves, as we work to do the practical work of love.

Religion as a River

Although we can see similarities like this between Christianity and Hinduism, Nick Sutton, professor of Hindu studies at Oxford, reminds his students, the question "What do Hindus believe?" can never be answered simply, because "the Hindu identity is not a single thing. . . . Many people, Hindus and non-Hindus alike, find it difficult to appreciate this diversity and hence find Hinduism very confusing, but it is only when diversity, distinction, and difference are accepted and appreciated that the Hindu identity begins to make any sense at all."[56]

Celtic spirituality can be equally confusing. The Celtic Evangelical Christian, the Celtic Nature mystic, and the Celtic Pagan may share some beliefs and attitudes in common, but they also are very different from one another. In a similar way, the modern expression of Celtic spirituality may be inspired by the stories and writings of the ancient Celts, but at the same time, it is a very different way of life from what the ancient Celtic followers of Jesus practiced in the sixth century (which in turn is different from the Celtic Christianity of the later Middle Ages). Today's variations of Celtic spirituality, like modern versions of Hinduism, are often interpretations of ancient ideas that suit the needs and desires of the modern world.

Human beings have a tendency to reduce religions (as well as people, nations, political parties, and even animals) to monolithic stereotypes. We pick out a few characteristics and focus on them. We picture a religion as though it were a single, immense stone; cut that stone open, and we assume you'll find pretty much the same composition of minerals everywhere you look. The stone may wear down, ever so slowly, thanks to erosion, but its nature changes very little. This perspective on religion leads to sweeping generalizations that leave out the lovely detail and variation of individuals' actual beliefs.

In reality, religions are more like rivers than stones: constantly flowing, responding to and shaped by the environments around them, changing directions as needed, ebbing and flowing with the passage of time. We may resist religious change, seeing it as a threat to the "true faith"—or we can see change as part of the ongoing Divine revelation, a revelation that is always expanding yet always incomplete.

Hinduism is the world's oldest living religion, practiced today by millions of people, so it makes sense that it manifests in many different variations. Hindus themselves have no problem with these inconsistencies, for they believe that no single religion teaches the only way to salvation above all others. Instead, from a Hindu perspective, all genuine paths are facets of the Divine Light, deserving tolerance and understanding.

According to the Hindu American Foundation,

> The Hindu world has been able to embrace the reality of diversity through its philosophy of pluralism. Every being, with their varying likes and dislikes, their unique personalities, and their different cultures, not only connect with one another in their own unique ways, but connect with the Divine in their own

individual ways. As such, Hindus understand the Divine (existence, pure being, light of consciousness) to: 1) Manifest in different forms; 2) Be understood and worshipped by various means; 3) Speak to each individual in different ways to enable them to not only believe in the Divine, but experience and know the Divine.[57]

An American Hindu monastery's website explains: "We Hindus believe in the one all-pervasive God who energizes the entire universe. We can see [Divinity] in the life shining out of the eyes of humans and all creatures."[58] As we mentioned in the previous chapter, this view of God as being within all things is called panentheism.

Panentheism Versus Theism and Pantheism

As religious scholar Nancy Frackenberry summarized, "For classical theism, the God-question in an age of science is the question of whether, in addition to everything else that exists, there also exists [a Divine] entity."[59] This perspective sees God as something extra, something that stands separate from the world we perceive with our physical senses.

Theologians often speak about the relationship between God and Creation in terms of immanence or transcendence—presence or distance—and traditional theists believe God is transcendent, beyond and distant from the world we experience; if the Divine intervenes in that world at all, it is from outside, in acts of supernatural power. Pantheism, on the other hand, focuses on immanence and presence: God and the tangible world are virtually identical.

Panentheism combines these two perspectives: God is in the world and the world is in God, but God is also more than the world. Panentheism believes the Divine Spirit intersects every aspect of physical life—and at the same time extends beyond it. All reality is contained in a Spirit that lies *both* beyond it *and* within it. According to a three-thousand-year-old Vedic scripture, creation constitutes one-quarter of the Divine, while three-quarters of the Divine Spirit remain in a timeless realm.[60]

Since the Divine Spirit "energizes the entire universe," all experiences—interactions with co-workers, standing in line at a store, going to the theater, or embracing a lover—are opportunities to interact with the Divine. If we see the Beloved shining out of the eyes of every living creature, we can learn to view even unpleasant people as lanterns of the Divine Flame. Leaves and trees and all growing things are the garments of our greening God. Everything is sacred. If we navel gaze, the Beloved is there, within our own minds and hearts; if we peer through the lens of the Hubble space telescope, the Beloved is there—and beyond.

Panentheism also lies at the heart of Celtic Christianity, in both its ancient and modern forms. Saint Ninian's Catechism, an eighth-century document explaining the rudiments of Christian faith for new Celtic believers, says, "Perceive the eternal Word of God reflected in every plant and insect, every bird and animal, and every man and woman."[61] John Scotus Eriugena, the most influential Celtic theologian of the early Middle Ages, taught panentheism, declaring, in effect, "The whole of reality is God."[62]

Ideas and experiences are not the same, of course. Sarvepalli Radhakrishnan, an important twentieth-century Hindu intellectual, insisted that Hinduism, unlike many forms of Western religion, is a religion based on personal experience, rather than beliefs and dogma. "We are not saved by creeds," he said.[63] Panentheism may remain a mere intellectual concept, an interesting idea to play with, but experiencing this concept for ourselves—*living it,* rather than merely thinking about it—opens doors to transformation. Up until now, we have explored the *what*; for the rest of the chapter, we will delve into *how*.

Four Great Paths to God

When you hear the word *yoga,* you might think of sculpted limbs in spandex contorted in unbelievable ways in some posh studio. Many of us don't realize that in the big picture of Hindu spirituality, this Westernized, physical-type yoga is a small branch of the yoga family tree.

Over many centuries, Hindus, yearning for ways to experience the Divine Presence more directly, developed various practices by which to seek God; all these spiritual practices come under the heading of *yoga.* Yogic practices were designed to enable humans to reach union with God; they are the disciplines needed to attain spiritual growth.

The word *yoke* comes from the same common root as the word *yoga*, meaning "to unite." In Hinduism, yoga is the means—the experience, the *how*—by which we unite the Divine Spirit who lives within us with the all-pervading, transcendent Spirit (Brahman).[64] We can view Jesus' words through a Hindu lens when he says, "Take my yoke upon you, and learn from me. . . . For my yoke is easy, and my burden is light" (Matt. 11:29–30). In other words, Jesus offers a yoga path to God.

Over time, Hinduism grouped its spiritual practices into four main paths to enlightenment. Modern practitioners say that the four great paths correspond to four major spiritual personality types, so each individual's journey to God is a matter of discerning their yogic type.[65] This accords with the Spanish mystic Saint John of the Cross, who wrote that spiritual directors should seek "not to guide souls by a way suitable to themselves but to ascertain the way that God himself is pointing them."[66] Both perspectives affirm that each of us can discover "a way suitable" for ourselves and seek after God in that way. Connection with the Divine is not a one-size-fits-all construct.

Maybe you have done personality profiles such as the Myer Briggs personality test or the Enneagram. Or maybe you've been tested to determine your best learning modality—audio, visual, or tactile. If so, you know the value of tailoring growth experiences to your personality type. In a similar way, as you read each of the following descriptions of the four yoga paths, ask yourself whether it describes you. Understanding your unique spiritual personality and pairing that with the appropriate path can be like wind in your spiritual sails.

Jnana: The Path to God Through Knowledge

Jnana (pronounced something like "nyana") is a Sanskrit word that translates as "knowledge"; it is the pathway to God via interior reflection. Do you love to read books about spiritual growth, scriptures, or the nature of the universe? Do you listen to podcasts or talk shows that teach you about life? If knowledge lights you up, you may be best suited to the jnana path.

The way Hinduism sees religious knowledge is not the same, however, as the way Western seekers (at least during the past five centuries) have pursued spiritual studies, seeking to establish precise interpretations. Hindu sages take a flexible approach to reading sacred texts; they are open to symbolic and metaphorical insights. The ancient Celtic way of sacred study likewise beckons each reader to a multifaceted view. In his book *Periphyseon*, ninth-century Irish theologian John Scotus Eriugena writes, "For there are many ways, indeed an infinite number, of interpreting the Scriptures, just as in one and the same feather of a peacock and even in the same small portion of a feather, we see a marvelous beautiful variety of innumerable colors."[67] In other words, sacred scriptures shouldn't act as blinders that narrow your field of vision but more like a kaleidoscope, expanding your vision into diverse patterns of Divine reality. Thinking of each spiritual text as a peacock's tail feather, filled with manifold possibilities, has renewed my love for these holy writings.

Sacred reading can become a sort of epiphany—an experience of God's presence. The Eleventh Teaching of the Bhagavad Gita, a Hindu religious epic, contains a mind-opening passage that has led many readers to sense the nearness of Divine glory. In it, Krishna tells Arjuna, the warrior-prince at the heart of the story:

> *By hundreds and then by thousands,*
> *behold, Arjuna, my manifold celestial forms*
> *of innumerable shapes and colors.*
> *Behold the gods of the sun,*
> *and those fire and light;*
> *the gods of storm and lightning,*
> *and the two luminous charioteers of heaven.*
> *Behold, descendant of Bharata, marvels never seen before.*
> *See now the whole universe*

with all things that move and move not
and whatever thy soul may yearn to see.
See it all as One in me.
But though thou never canst see me
with these they mortal eyes:
I will give thee divine sight.
Behold my wonder and glory.[68]

Celtic monks, Spirit-inspired, created similar passages of brilliant epiphany. Consider the beginning of "The Ever-New Tongue," composed in Ireland in the ninth or tenth century:

In the beginning God created heaven and earth.'
The High King of the world,
who is mightier than every king,
who is loftier than every power,
who is fiercer than every dragon,
who is gentler than every child,
who is brighter than suns,
who is holier than every elder,
who is more vengeful than men,
who is more loving than every mother,
the only Son of God the Father,
bestowed this account upon the many
peoples of the world.[69]

Have you ever read something that—to use an expression popular in the 1960s—blew your mind? If you can't think of one, then perhaps you should search for sacred texts with which you are unfamiliar—or perhaps reread familiar scriptures with your eyes opened wider, so you see past traditional interpretations. Inspired books, the gifts of enlightened scholar-saints, offer experiences of Divine union transmitted by pen and ink, which can become, for the reader, shortcuts along the *jnana* road. As we learn from the spiritual insights and experiences of others, we may be empowered to break through the veil of *Maya* and encounter God more from the heart than the head. If we seek a deeper connection with the Divine, we would do well to seek such literary epiphanies.

Bhakti: The Path to God Through Adoration

The bhakti path (pronounced something like "buck-tea") is the path to God through acts of devotion. Hindus on this path engage in ritual practices of worship, or *puja*, at home altars or public temples. These practices involve singing, chanting, and offering incense, perfumes, or flowers in the symbolic presence of the Divine. For Christians in liturgical traditions, the bhakti path might mean celebrating the Eucharist or praying with censors and icons. Some Christians engage in similar heart-worship when they sing worship songs with uplifted hands or kneel in fervent prayer at the altar.

Do you love to worship God, alone or with a congregation? Do you find that religious acts of devotion ignite deep emotions within you? Would you rather love God with your feelings than understand God with your mind? Those are signals urging you forward on the path of adoration.

It's funny how we do—or don't—display emotions in different settings. I know some religious people who don't like to display emotion at their church because "we don't want to look like fanatics" but later in the same afternoon will jump up and down (literally) and scream at the TV in their living room when their favorite team makes a goal or gets hit with a penalty. By contrast, God-seekers on the bhakti path are willing to wear their hearts on their sleeves, their love for God more ardent than love for any sports team or political cause.

Music and Poetry

As countless love songs attest, when we love someone, we want to express our feelings with words and music. Hinduism has a rich tradition of poetry and music as essential to the worship experience, because it both arouses our physical senses and creates spiritual vibrations that enhance our sense of connection with the Divine.[70] According to Hindu journalist Syama Allard,

> Sound vibrations are said to have the ability to awaken our original spiritual consciousness and help us remember that we are beyond the dualities of life, and actually originate from the Divine. As such, the main goal of many types of Hindu musical expression is to help stir us out of our spiritual slumber by evoking feelings of love and connection that help us to better perceive the presence of the Divine within all.[71]

Jews and Christians also have an ancient heritage of sacred song. Both traditions have understood the erotic poetry in the Bible's Song of Songs as the soul's longing for Divine union:

> *Let him kiss me with the kisses of his mouth!*
> *For your love is better than wine;*
> *your anointing oils are fragrant;*
> *your name is perfume poured out;*
> *therefore the maidens love you.*

Draw me after you; let us make haste.
(Song of Songs 1:1–4).

For thousands of years, people have recited, chanted, and sung the psalms to express their heart-love for God. Psalms like this one were particularly important to the early Celtic followers of Christ:

It is good to give thanks to the Lord,
to sing praises to your name, O Most High;
to declare your steadfast love in the morning,
and your faithfulness by night,
to the music of the lute and the harp,
to the melody of the lyre.
For you, O Lord, have made me glad by your work;
at the works of your hands I sing for joy.
(Psalm 92:1–4)

Celtic monks and saints constantly prayed and sang the Psalms throughout their day and at set times of worship.

In the nineteenth century, folklorist Alexander Carmichael recorded the spiritual chants and songs that Highland farmers and fishermen sang as they went about their tasks. These songs often showed devotion to God:

God with me lying down,
God with me rising up,
God with me in each ray of light,
and I have no ray of joy without God.[72]

Pilgrimage

Has a geographically distant loved one ever delighted you by showing up unannounced for a birthday or anniversary, proving the extent of their love by traveling so far to see you? In a similar way, religious pilgrims express their love for God by journeying to sacred sites; they encounter God both on the way and at their destination.

Bhaktis in India have made pilgrimages for thousands of years. The *Kumbh Mela* ("festival of the sacred pitcher"), for example, is the largest pilgrimage on Earth, during which millions of travelers take a dip in one of India's sacred rivers. As one Hindu practitioner explains, "Pilgrim places serve as God's foot prints upon earth. . . . They also serve as power houses, radiating enormous sacred energy, and thereby contribute to the spiritual wellbeing of the people and the community." These spiritual journeys, also, according to the same Hindu, help pilgrims break free from daily routines, allowing them to practice the renunciation of this world's comforts that's necessary for spiritual growth. Pilgrimage is an opportunity to both practice spiritual self-discipline and experience the Divine more intensely.[73]

Likewise, the Celtic lands hold many "thin places"—like Hinduism's "power houses" of sacred energy—that have drawn throngs of itinerant worshippers since the Middle Ages. Celtic pilgrim destinations include the Holy Islands of Iona and Lindisfarne; the Holy Grail town of Glastonbury; the remains of Saints Oswald, Cuthbert, and Bede at Durham Cathedral; and Downpatrick Cathedral, the burial place of Ireland's greatest saints, Patrick and Brigid. For the early Celtic Christ-followers, however, the destination was not as important as the journey; pilgrimage was seen as the central metaphor for our lifelong journey to God. Even while pilgrims were at home in whatever locations they found themselves—for God is everywhere—they also understood that we live in perpetual exile from our true Home; the outward journey of a pilgrimage reflects the inner spiritual process of transformation. Like Hindu pilgrims, Celtic pilgrims who exiled themselves from the comforts of home also taught themselves to rely only on God.

Ultimately, pilgrimage is a journey of love. If you walk the bhakti path, pilgrimage is one more way to both find and express intimacy with the Divine. Practitioners of bhakti know the Beatles had it right: "All you need is love."

Karma: The Path to God Through Unselfish Actions

The third path to God, karma yoga, is through practical service. Where jnana yoga is for intellectuals, and bhakti yoga is for lovers, karma yoga works best for individuals given to physical activity. In any church or temple, there are always some folks who are constantly moving—serving meals at the soup kitchen, fixing the building's air conditioner, cleaning the floors, polishing the furniture. Maybe that's you—the person more comfortable with a hammer, a mixing bowl, or a needle in hand than a prayer book. If so, you may be a karmic yogi. These individuals are proof that the Beloved can be found in the world of everyday affairs as easily as anywhere. Karmic actions must always, however, be done without thought of reward.

Many Westerners have a simplistic understanding of karma: the idea that what goes around comes around. In other words, if you do a good deed, then God or the Universe will surely reward you—but if you stab someone in the back, then you better watch your own back. The eyes of a true karma disciple are fixed on a greater prize. Krishna tells his karma yogis in the Bhagavad Gita: "Whatever you do, whatever you eat, whatever you offer in sacrifice, whatever you give, whatever austerity you practice . . . do this as an offering to Me."[74] Union with the Supreme Being is more important than receiving earthly rewards, so the karmic yogi acts without any concern for a worldly payback. In terms of Eastern and Celtic Christianity, the real goal of right actions is *theosis*—partaking of the Divine nature.

This Indian folktale illustrates karmic behavior: A yogi meditating on the banks of the Ganges sees a scorpion fall into the river. He scoops it out of the water, and it stings him, landing back in the water. He rescues it again, and it stings him again. A passerby asks the holy man, "Why do you keep rescuing that scorpion when its only gratitude is to bite you?" The yogi replies, "It is the nature of scorpions to bite. It is the nature of yogis to help others when they can."[75]

Today's challenges, such as the climate crisis, pandemic illnesses, or societal violence, can feel overwhelming. People are tempted to throw up their hands and quit caring: "We can't win so why even try?" The karma path shows another way: We continue to do what is right and good, even if our actions appear to be unrewarded. As Jesus told us:

> To you who hear I say, love your enemies, do good to those who hate you, bless those who curse you, pray for those who mistreat you. . . . Give to everyone who asks of you, and from the one who takes what is yours do not demand it back. Do to others as you would have them do to you. For if you love those who love you, what credit is that to you?

Even sinners love those who love them. And if you do good to those who do good to you, what credit is that to you? Even sinners do the same. If you lend money to those from whom you expect repayment, what credit [is] that to you? Even sinners lend to sinners, and get back the same amount. But rather, love your enemies and do good to them, and lend expecting nothing back." (Luke 6:28, 30–35)

Brigid of Kildare, Ireland, was a fifth-century master of karmic practice who was always expending physical energy to bless others. While, according to tradition, Brigid had many mystical experiences (such as serving as Mary's doula at the time of Jesus' birth), she was also constantly at work in the practical world of hungry bellies and thirsty mouths. She milked cows, churned butter, and served up abundant meals to anyone who was hungry. She was also a brewer who said she longed to serve a "great lake of ale for the King of Kings; I would wish the family of heaven to be drinking it throughout life and time."[76] Brigid reminds us that sweaty and stained hands can touch God as readily as those clasped in prayer.

Raja: The Path to God
Through Spiritual Exercises

Do you love to meditate? Do you find yourself drawn to places and times of quiet where you touch God in the stillness and explore the recesses of your own soul? You may be best suited "the royal road" of raja.

The raja path affirms that techniques such as meditation and hatha (body pose) movements are vital to spiritual growth. Raja means "royal," and Hindu tradition claims that this is the highest essence of the four yoga paths, the direct and most effectual route to the Divine. In the Bhagavad Gita, Krishna tells raja devotees: "If when a man leaves his earthly body he is in the silence of Yoga and, closing the doors of his soul, he keeps the mind in his heart . . . and remembering me utters OM . . . he goes to the path supreme. Those who in devotion of Yoga rest all their soul ever on me, very soon come unto me."[77]

Raja yoga has eight steps:

- *Yama:* self-control
- *Niyama:* self-discipline
- *Asana:* physical exercises
- *Pranayama:* breath exercises

- *Pratyahara*: withdrawal of the senses from external objects
- *Dharana:* concentration
- *Dhyana:* meditation
- *Samadhi:* complete union with the Divine

The final step of raja yoga, its ultimate goal, is to achieve a constant awareness of God's presence. The word *samadhi* can be broken down like this: *sam* (meaning "together with") + *adhi* (the "Supreme One") = the state in which the mind is completely absorbed in God.

In the seventeenth century, Brother Lawrence described this state of mind and heart: "For me, prayer is nothing more than a sense of God's presence, and overwhelming awareness of divine love. This awareness continues uninterrupted, both in prayer times and throughout the day."[78]

Hindus have great respect for *sadhus* (male) or *sadhvis* (female), people who have renounced worldly possessions, careers, and social relationships, in order to follow the raja path unencumbered by distractions. The word *sadhu* means "leading straight to the goal"[79] (which is the literal original meaning of the English word *righteous*), and sadhus and sadhvis don't mess around in their seeking after God. These spiritual super-athletes own minimal clothing and sleep under tarps or outdoors. Some live as hermits in remote caves, mountains, or forests, practicing extraordinary spiritual exercises, such as smearing their bodies with ashes; fasting perpetually, subsisting on little more than water and nibbles of food; or remaining in one position for months at a time, cross-legged or with one arm raised in adoration.

If Celtic Christians in the early Middle Ages had been magically transported to India where they met sadhus and sadhvis, they would have exclaimed, "Kindred after our own hearts!" Celtic saints were also noted for some pretty extreme ascetic practices. Saint Columba's biographer Adomnan said the saint "was ceaselessly occupied with the untiring labors of fasts and vigils, day and night, any of which works would seem to be humanly impossible."[80] Irish monasteries were established in wave-lashed, rocky places such as Skellig Michael, because such environments were deemed inhabitable; eking out each day's survival was a form of self-denial. According to tradition, Saint Kevin held his arm in an upright position until a baby bird hatched on it; he also slept during Lent and Advent seasons in a tiny cave overhanging the waters of a lake, with barely room to sit upright. Saints Kevin, David, and Cuthbert were known as "water men" because of their practice of praying through the night while standing in cold lakes or the ocean. Some monks and hermits subsisted on little more than water and herbs.

Of course, it is possible to experience God's presence without ascetic practices, as Brother Lawrence, who communed with God while working in the kitchen, would have affirmed. At the same time, perhaps we should consider: If the sadhus and Celtic saints went overboard in mortification, might we be going further overboard in privileged and materialistic excesses?

In any case, ascetic practices have no value in and of themselves. They are only useful in so far as they bring us into union with the Divine. And, as the Celtic monk Columba Marmion pointed out, this union "admits of a vast number of degrees." Marmion quotes Saint Ambrose, who wrote, "God is everywhere present but Divinity is nearest to those who love God," and then Marmion goes on to say that even as we find God and experience union with the Divine, we continue throughout our lives to endlessly seek still deeper intimacy and union.[81] Ascetic practices can contribute to this lifelong quest.

What Is *Your* Path?

This is a good time to ponder: *Which path to God best fits my own personality?* Take some time to consider this question. Then, the remainder of this chapter is grouped according to these four yoga paths. Choose which unique pattern best suits your spiritual style.

JNANA
DISCUSSION QUESTIONS
& SPIRITUAL PRACTICES

Go online and peruse the pages of the Book of Kells or the Lindisfarne Gospels. Do so playfully. What images strike you? Excite you? Mystify you?

Read the Bhagavad Gita, the most popular Hindu devotional text. Note in your journal any lines or phrases that particularly speak to you.

If you need to reinvigorate your study of scripture, consider the ancient Celtic way of reading and interpreting the Bible, which never limits scripture to its literal meanings but instead, weaves together multiple perspectives to reveal deeper, multifaceted truths. *The Peacock's Tail Feathers* (published by Anamchara

Books) is my guide to restarting your relationship with the Bible.

Spend some time journaling and reflecting on your relationship with scripture. Have there been times when it was especially precious to you or, conversely, times when it has been problematic? Considering that scripture remains the same, what changes in your perceptions caused these differing perspectives? How would you describe your relationship to scripture today?

Consider the Bible as a source of interspiritual wisdom. The Bible is sometimes presented as exclusive of other religious beliefs, and some portions of it read that way, but the Hebrew and Christian scriptures invite wider vistas of understanding. The Hebrew Bible contains material derived from the beliefs of Israel's non-Jewish neighbors. The Ark of the Covenant was modeled on the portable shrines found in Egyptian temples.[82] When the psalmist writes that God "broke the heads of the dragons in the waters" and "crushed the heads of Leviathan" (Psalm 74:13-14) he was referring to a myth borrowed from the Mesopotamian nations.[83]

We also find interspiritual influence in the Christian scripture. The Gospel of John illustrates Christ's Divine nature using the words of a non-Jewish mystic who lived five centuries before Christ: "In the beginning was the Word, and the Word was with God, and the Word was God. . . . All things came into being through him." (John 1:1–3). The "Word" in John 1 is *logos* in Greek, a term coined by the pagan philosopher Heraclitus. He believed that "all things are in process, and nothing stays still, we cannot step twice in the same river," yet while everything changes, in the Logos "all things are one."[84] John presents Christ as Heraclitus' *logos*.

Chapter 17 of the Acts of the Apostles tells of the apostle Paul to the Athenians that God created diverse humanity and "allotted the times of their existence and the boundaries of the places where they would live, so that they would search for God and perhaps fumble about for him and find him—though indeed he is not far from each one of us" (26-27). I love the idea of "fumbling" after God; it's such a great description of my own spiritual life. As we fumble through the scriptures and recognize them as invitations to interspiritual insights, may we connect more intimately with the One who indeed is not far from each of us.

Sit outdoors and read from the Psalms. How does a natural location affect your experience of scripture?

Take a psalm or another portion of scripture and rewrite it, inserting your name into the text wherever it has "people," "they," "brothers and sisters," etc. How does that change the impact of the Word for you?

Practice *lectio divina* with a favorite scripture text. Here is one set of instructions for doing so:

- *Read* the passage out loud.

- *Meditate:* Read the passage a second time. Listen for a word or phrase that speaks to you.

- *Pray:* Read the passage a third time. Reflect on how God may be speaking to you through that word or phrase.

- *Contemplate:* Read the passage a fourth time. Reflect on how God may be calling you to act through the word or phrase that spoke to you.

- *Act:* Close with a prayer of gratitude and ask for insight as to how you can actively respond to God's invitation.

BHAKTI
DISCUSSION QUESTIONS
& SPIRITUAL PRACTICES

Play a favorite worship song—on an instrument if you are so able or on a recorded format. Sing along or just listen. Think of God as your lover sitting near you while you express adoration.

Visit an open church or temple. Pray or offer a candle or incense privately to God, who is alone with you at this spot.

Do you live near a "thin place" where you sense God's Presence in a special way? Take a day trip—a small pilgrimage—to visit this place (a nearby shrine, holy well, grotto, waterfall, or wherever you particularly sense Divinity).

Find a picture of the most beautiful place you have ever seen. Thank God for revealing Divinity in that vision of beauty.

If you have quit going to church or temple, let go of any guilt. A great many people have done the same. But try an experiment as you watch some online services: is there one that draws you? Then consider attending a similar in-person worship experience that seems interesting. You don't have to pal around with people: You can enter the service a bit late and leave a bit early. Just see if you can enjoy the music, rituals, or message. Look for a tiny whisper of God's Presence within this very flawed human setting.

Write God a love letter.

In a journal, write down whatever strikes you as a "God thing."

Sit or stand in a wild place that pleases you. Note everything your senses take in: sights, smells, sounds. Thank God for each distinct sensory impression.

Thank God for everything around you. Be exhaustive and creative.

Search for animal life: birds, seals, sheep, or pets. Talk to God about each creature: what is lovely, admirable, surprising, or pleasing about each creature you see?

Watch people (discretely!). Look at faces, eyes, body language. Silently thank God for each unique image of the Divine.

"Read" the land as "God's first book." This is from Bruce Stanley's wonderful book *Forest Church: A Field*

Guide to Spiritual Connection with Nature (available from Anamchara Books). Pick a natural location and ask yourself:

1. What forces of Nature (God's providence) have shaped the features of this landscape?

2. What natural elements of this landscape might have struck people in the past as especially holy or sacred?

3. What artifacts of human habitation might attest to the holiness or sacredness of the land?

4. Try to imagine the place through God's age-less lens.

5. Thank God for all that God has done, is doing, and will do, through this piece of Earth.

Go to an art museum that contains sacred art. For each work of art, try to imagine the person who crafted it and what their day-to-day life was like. How did they experience Divinity? What can you learn from their creative vision? While you are at the art museum, compare Eastern and Western forms of sacred art. What does this comparison say to you about the Divine?

Read *The Four Agreements* by Don Miguel Ruiz. It might help you to love yourself more—and loving yourself more, you may find it easier to love both other people and God. Remember, when Jesus gave us the "greatest commandment," he connected our love of God and "neighbor" with loving ourselves (Matthew 22:37, 39).

Consider these questions:

- In what ways are you comfortable showing your love to other human beings?

- Could your ways of loving other mortals extend to loving God? If not, why not? And if so, how so?

- When have you felt God's love for you? Have you found certain places, activities, or times to be especially conducive to your awareness of Divine love? How might you make more room in your life for these times, places, and actions?

- How can you praise God with your voice—by playing an instrument, singing acapella, or singing along with music? If you're not comfortable doing this with other people, you can still feel free to offer love songs to God. Do you have favorite hymns or worship songs?

- When do you feel most alive? What people, places, things, and activities contribute to that feeling.

- When does God seem most real to you? Is there any connection between this answer and the answer to the previous set of questions?

KARMA
DISCUSSION QUESTIONS
& SPIRITUAL PRACTICES

Can you remember a time someone did something wonderful for you without expecting or demanding any reward? Say a prayer of thanksgiving for that. Consider expressing your gratitude to the other person as well, as an email, a text message, a note in the mail, or in spoken words.

When is the last time you did anything without any thought or expectation of reward? How did this make you feel? What motivated you? Did you feel God tugging at you? Was there some ego involved? Were you thanked or not? How did you respond to being thanked or not? What did you learn from this experience that might be helpful next time a similar opportunity arises? Journal your answers to these questions.

How do you react to the scorpion story earlier in this chapter? Why do you have that reaction?

How do you use your physical strength for good? Think of a way you can literally put some muscle into a philanthropic activity.

Are there past actions for which you need to seek forgiveness? Are you part of a group that needs to ask forgiveness or make restitution for past harms? Make concrete plans—right now, don't delay—and put steps in place to ensure you do it.

Ask God to lead you to someone to whom you can lend a helping hand today, motivated only by compassion and respect.

Give someone an anonymous gift. Make sure there's no way they'll find out you are the giver. How does that feel? Can you just forget that you did it? Or do you find yourself "stroking" your ego over your action? Be curious, rather than judgmental, about your reactions.

Volunteer at a community garden, soup kitchen, repair shop, hospital, or roadside cleanup—someplace you can use your muscles for good.

RAJA
DISCUSSION QUESTIONS
& SPIRITUAL PRACTICES

Do you have a routine spiritual practice?

When is the best time for you to pray or meditate? When you first wake up, during your lunch break, before going to bed at night, or some other time during the day?

Is there a spiritual practice you've neglected and wish to resume?

Is there a spiritual practice you are curious about and would like to start?

Is it easier to follow a spiritual practice routine by yourself or with a group? Is there a group you could join?

What routine has enabled you to experience the most spiritual growth?

Is there a routine that is holding back or harming your spiritual growth?

Have you ever experienced an epiphany—a mystical moment—while doing a spiritual practice? What elements might have helped that experience to happen?

Take a lesson in prayer from Mahatma Gandhi:

> *Take the Name* with every breath. When a child, my nurse taught me to repeat Ramanama (the name of God) whenever I felt afraid, and it has been second nature with me. I may even say the word is in my heart, if not actually on my lips, all the twenty-four hours. A Christian may find the same solace from the repetition of the name of Jesus. Only the repetition must not be a lip-expression, but part of your very being.[85]

Practice "fixed-point" meditation. Pick a natural object, a painting, a statue, or some other object of devotion. Sit and focus your gaze and your attention on just this one point.

Practice breath prayer. In the words of Anthony De Mello:

> Become aware of your breathing for a while. Now reflect on the presence of God in the

atmosphere all around you . . . reflect on [God's] presence in the air you are breathing . . . Be conscious of [Divine] presence in the air as you breathe in and out . . . now express yourself to God. But do this nonverbally, not through words but through your breathing. First of all, express great yearning: "My God, I long for you." Just by the way you breathe. Now express trust or surrender. "I surrender myself entirely to you." . . . by breathing. Continue to express yourself to God nonverbally.[86]

Read and do the practices in *Sadhana, A Way to God* by Anthony De Mello. It is a complete course in meditative practice by a Christian priest whose faith was enhanced by Hindu techniques.

In Hindi tradition, people pray with *mala* beads. In a similar way, the Desert Fathers and Mothers and Celtic monks used prayer cords. Find a length of cord about 16 inches long and tie knots an inch apart. Then, as you touch each knot, pray a mantra, such as "Abba" or "Deep Peace,"

Procure a piece of spiritual art, either printed or on a screen. Meditate on the image: Trace it with your finger, imagine going within the image, and seek to see Spirit in the artwork.

Pray about how to open yourself more completely to the Divine. In stillness, listen and look for any word or direction that comes to you.

3

CELTIC SPIRITUALITY AND BUDDHISM

Paths to Peace

Now today, it is quite clear,
that all major religious traditions,
in spite of different philosophy,
different ways of approach,
they all carry the same message,
a message of love, compassion, forgiveness. . . .

—His Holiness the Dalai Lama
(speaking in 2011 at St. Brigid's Parish Church
in Kildare, Ireland)

When I lived in northern Arizona, I often took visitors to the Amitabha Stupa and Peace Park in Sedona. Just outside the town, at the end of the paved streets, visitors park their cars and climb up trails over ruddy stone slopes and past juniper trees, quietly ascending until they reach the main stupa. Prayer flags converge from all directions and meet at the top of the immense monument, its pinkish colors blending with the surrounding red-rock hillside. People of all sorts come there, some Buddhist, others from a wide variety of backgrounds. They walk in silence thrice around the central pillar, rotate massive prayer wheels, or sit at a nearby shaded area in meditation.

The builders and caretakers of the site say the thousands of prayer scrolls inserted into the base of the stupa generate waves of healing energy that reach out miles in every direction. You don't have to believe that to feel the peace this place generates. I've taken many guests there over the years and listed the Peace Park as a self-guided field trip for my comparative religions students—and I never heard a guest or student express disappointment after visiting the stupa; the place conveys a real feeling of inner serenity.

Many people attest that the teachings of the Buddha offer a pathway toward inward peace, which then flows outward in a ripple effect of reconciliation with circumstances and people. Christ-followers committed to the ways of peace can find wisdom, encouragement, and inspiration in the Buddha's insights.

Jesus and Buddha: Brothers in the Quest for Peace

In the introduction to Marcus Borg's book *Jesus and Buddha: The Parallel Sayings*, Buddhist scholar Jack Kornfield includes a fascinating memory. During the Vietnam War, he visited an island monastery in the Mekong Delta where a Buddhist teacher known as the Coconut Monk lived. Kornfield came to a hilltop and beheld two fifty-foot statues, one of Buddha, the other of Christ. The two statues had their arms around each other's shoulders.

Kornfield writes, "While helicopter gunships flew by overhead and war raged around us, Buddha and Jesus stood there like brothers, expressing compassion and healing for all who would follow their way."[87] The anecdote proves an apt introduction to Borg's book, which is a powerful reflection on how Jesus and Buddha often seem to speak with one voice.

Becoming Enlightened

Siddhartha Gautama was not yet known as the Buddha when he was born around 500 BCE, in Lumbini on the India-Nepal border: He was a pampered rich kid whose royal father did not wish him to experience any suffering, so he spoiled Gautama. Then, as a young man, Gautama escaped the palace, where for the first time, he beheld old age, sickness, death, and poverty. These experiences shook him to his soul. Seeking to cope with this new awareness of suffering, he left behind palace and privilege.

Gautama wandered for years, attempting to find the secret of a contented life. He studied under renowned masters and fasted to the extreme, but the truth eluded him. Finally, he sat down under a tree, resolved to find

the key to mastering the challenges of human suffering. The demon king Mara appeared to him, presenting temptations similar to those the devil flung at Christ during his forty days in the desert before he began his ministry (Matthew 4:1–11). Like Christ, Gautama overcame each test. After many days of going inward, perceiving miraculous things, Gautama roared and leapt to his feet, ready to proclaim a better way to live. He was now the Buddha, meaning "one who is awake."

The Buddha's teaching spread throughout Asia and—at least in the form of rumors and hints—as far as Europe. Archeologists have found a sixth-century bronze Buddha in Sweden (alongside an elaborate crozier—part of a bishop's staff—from Ireland).[88] Ancient buddha statues have also been found in Irish bogs, indicating that by the seventh century, a well-read Irish monk could have known about Buddhism. Then, in the early twentieth century, leaders in the Celtic Renaissance began to discern a "Celtishness" in Buddhism and embraced that as an alternative to the English rule and church strictures of their time. Since the 1970s, Buddhism has grown rapidly in Ireland.[89]

Marketing analysts reported that in 2022, Americans spent over 502 million dollars on self-help books. Thousands of years before this flood of self-improvement advice, the Buddha freely shared four principles that rank among humanity's greatest self-help guides. These Four Noble Truths can be explained in minutes but take a lifetime to live.

The Four Noble Truths

The First Noble Truth: Life Is Characterized by Dukkha (Unease)

Life is rarely perfect. After an extravagantly expensive dream wedding, the newlyweds and the entire wedding party become ill with COVID-19. A fantasy vacation to an exotic tropical island devolves into a rash of painful bugbites and sunburn. A promotion you dreamed about for years turns out to be a job you really don't like. As the Buddha declared, "Life is *dukkha*."

Dukkha literally means "wobbly wheel" and can be translated as "uneasy," "difficult," or, more colloquially, "shit happens." In the time of the Buddha, wheel axles had no ball bearings, and metal axles were expensive. Carts' wooden axles rubbed against wooden holes, and the resulting friction quickly wore them down. The carts still got people from place to place, but it was a bumpy ride. Like life.

The Buddha's way is sometimes misunderstood as pessimism, considering life's cup to be always half empty rather than half full. In fact, the Buddha presented the Four Noble Truths as *liberation* rather than hopelessness. Freed from negative emotions such as anger, fear, and disappointment, we can experience life's deepest joys. Have you noticed how often the Dalai Lama is chuckling or seen the jolly grin on some Chinese statues of the Buddha? Buddhism isn't negative in its outlook.

A Buddhist teacher told me, "Imagine a hat rack with many pegs. Each hat on the rag is an emotion. A master can pick up whatever emotion she chooses to wear and put that on." Doesn't that sound like a glorious freedom? I must admit, I'm far from living that. I still get irritated when tasks pile up, angry when insulted, or fearful when threatened. But if I apply the Buddha's core principles, events lose their sting. Attending a Buddhist group on weeknights over the course of several years, I found that conversations on the application of the Noble Truths helped translate the principles into daily life. I haven't yet achieved "pick up whatever emotion you choose and put it on," but I can now more readily recognize and address my emotions.

As self-help guru M. Scott Peck said in his book *The Road Less Traveled*, "Life is difficult. This is a great truth, one of the greatest truths. It is a great truth because once we truly see this truth, we transcend it. Once we truly know that life is difficult—once we truly understand and accept it—then life is no longer difficult."[90]

The First Noble Truth is a healthy counterbalance to the oft-herd emphasis on the "goodness of Creation" in Celtic spirituality. The ancient Welsh theologian Pelagius taught "original goodness" (as opposed to "original sin"), yet he was fully aware of how sinful choices inject pain and suffering into God's good world. In his letter *On the Christian Life*, Pelagius warns: "Hear what is said to those who love this world and who vaunt themselves and are satisfied in this present time: 'Do you not know that friendship with the world is enmity with God? Therefore, whoever wishes to be a friend of the world makes himself an enemy of God' (James 4:4)."[91] At the same time, the Celtic saints saw the Celestial Monarch's goodness filling each nook and cranny of a Divinely ordered world. Among the saints and scholars of the Celtic lands were nondual thinkers able to grasp the both-and of Creation; Celtic Christianity affirms life is dukkha at the same time that the world is suffused with Divine glory.

The Second Noble Truth: Understanding the Cause of Unease (Attachments)

I invite you to take a minute for a little thought experiment. Grab a writing tool and paper and, quick as you can, write down things that make people happy. Don't overthink it—just write as many things as you can think of in a minute or less. Now review your list. I expect you included things such as family, food, romance, friendship, pets, good health, and so forth. Now go back over your list and cross out everything that can possibly change with time. For example, will you always have good food? It is not guaranteed: some people starve, others lose their sense of taste. Will you always enjoy being with your romantic partner? Countless country music songs offer proof to the contrary! Does *anything* on your list endure? The Second Noble Truth reminds us that despite our desire for permanence, everything changes. As the chorus of the 1970s hit by the rock band Kansas put it: "All we are is dust in the wind."

In one way or another, this realization is the source of all anxiety. We are attached to impermanent reality. We cling to things that inevitably change, and that attachment to transient things will doom us to unhappiness. Jesus expressed this by saying, "The cares of the world, and the lure of wealth, and the desire for other things come in and choke the word, and it yields nothing" (Mark 4:19).

The Celtic saints modeled their spiritual lives on the Egyptian Desert Fathers and Mothers, for whom "anxiety about the material circumstances of life—sex, food, money, irritations" was the bane of spirituality.[92] Desert Father Dorotheus of Gaza offered this practical advice:

> A man takes a little walk and sees something.
> His thoughts say to him, "Go over there and
> investigate" and he says to his thoughts, "No!
> I won't" and he cuts off his desire. Again he

finds someone gossiping and his thoughts say to him, "You go and have a word with them," and he cuts off his desire and does not speak. Or again his thoughts say to him, "Go and ask, the cook, what's cooking?" And he does not go but cuts off his desire. . . . A man denying himself in this way comes little by little to form a habit of it so that from denying himself in little things he begins to deny himself in great without the least trouble. Finally he comes not to have any of these extraneous desires but whatever happens to him he is satisfied with it as if it were the very thing he wanted.[93]

Anthony De Mello, whose faith was nourished by the wisdom in his homeland of India, explained attachments this way:

Has it ever struck you that you have been programmed to be unhappy? First your society and your culture taught you to believe that you would not be happy without certain persons and certain things . . . money, power, success, approval, a good reputation, love, friendship, spirituality . . . what is your particular combination?[94]

Do we possess our things, or do they possess us? Possessions are not always material. Could it be that you and I are subtly but strongly attached to qualities such as perfectionism, impressing others, or the need to be in control?

The Third Noble Truth: Freedom From Attachment

We only suffer as long as we resist what is. The key to freedom from unease is to enjoy people, experiences, and things on a nonattachment basis. As we accept that everything changes and let go of the falsehood that certain things have the power to make us happy or unhappy, we have greater liberty to love people and things thoroughly, on a nonattachment basis. In the process, we may come to experience more emotional freedom and joy.

De Mello offered a simple practice for freedom from attachments: "Pass in review now all those attachments of yours. And to each person or object that comes to mind say: 'I am not really attached to you at all. I am merely deluding myself into the belief that without you I will not be happy.'"[95] This is simple but amazingly powerful.

My favorite Buddhist parable tells of a person who has mastered detachment:

> A man traveling across a field encountered a tiger. He fled, the tiger after him. Coming to a precipice, he caught hold of the root of a wild vine and swung himself down over the edge. The tiger sniffed at him from above. Trembling, the man looked down to where, far below, another tiger was waiting to eat him. Only the vine sustained him. Two mice, one white and one black, little by little started to gnaw away the vine. The man saw a luscious strawberry near him. Grasping the vine with one hand, he plucked the strawberry with the other. How sweet it tasted![96]

That example is extreme: Personally, I don't know anyone who could be so detached in such a fix. But the story always makes me smile. My wife and I remind each other when we're in challenging situations: "Look for the strawberry."

Detachment does take work: It's a practice that needs to be relentlessly pursued. After you disentangle yourself from one emotional bond, another may present itself the next day. You can cut an attachment loose and get reentangled in short order. You'll probably never get to the point of saying, "I have no attachments"—but you can get to the point where you find yourself freer.

Cessation of attachments also brings to my mind an ancient Celtic baptismal font in the church in Eardisley, Herefordshire, on the Welsh border. Carved on the font in bold relief is a man who art experts say is Adam representing all humanity. Tendrils wrap around his entire body like the strangling appendages of some science-fiction monster. Meanwhile, Christ is pulling Adam free of these cords. The artist likely intended the entrapping tendrils to represent sinful inclinations, but I like to see them as attachments and imagine Christ seeking to free us all from their grip.

The Fourth Noble Truth: The Eightfold Path

The Buddha can be tricky: He gets us started by promising Four Noble Truths. That's easy—anyone can master four truths, right? But then he tells us the Fourth Noble Truth comes in an eight-part package. Since four plus eight equals twelve, the Buddha offered the first twelve-step program.

The eight paths contained within the Fourth Noble Truth are:

> right understanding
> right thought
> right speech
> right action
> right livelihood
> right effort
> right mindfulness
> right meditation[97]

Gautama Buddha began a monastic order during his lifetime based on his teachings, including the Eightfold Path. While the truths are universal and perfectly workable for laypeople, monks and nuns in monasteries were the ones who spread them and kept them alive. Likewise, the heart of Celtic Christianity was monastic.

Celtic monastic communities (male and female) had an "Order" or "Way of Life," which can be likened to Buddha's Eightfold Path. Although Protestants have traditionally eschewed monasticism, insisting with Luther that a farmer or butcher is as holy as a monk, contemporary Celtic Christianity—often birthed in Protestant contexts—continues to generate a variety of robust monastic (or "neomonastic") expressions. Listed below is the 'Way of Life' for the modern-day Community of Aidan and Hilda, a dispersed neomonastic community inspired by the lives of Aidan (the Irish monk who brought Christianity to England) and Hilda (the English abbess who spread the new faith among her people). The community's Way of Life is encapsulated in ten "Waymarks," which can be summarized as a set of questions. As you read them, take a moment to consider how they compare with the Buddha's Eightfold Path:

1. How am I seeking to *grow in knowledge*?

2. How do I experience *companionship* on my spiritual journey?

3. What is my personal *rhythm* of prayer, work, and rest?

4. What are my *guiding principles* in my use of money and possessions?

5. What steps do I take to *care for the environment*?

6. How do I help others find *healing*?

7. What do I do to enable the *Holy Spirit to guide* me?

8. How do I *support others* through prayer?

9. How do I show welcome and *hospitality* to other people?

10. How do I *help others to find faith* in Jesus?[98]

Buddha's Eightfold Path and the Celtic Christian Way of Life both ensure that faith is lived and not just professed. As Buddhist master Thich Nhat Hahn emphasized:

> A true teaching is not static. It is not mere words but the reality of life. Many who have neither the way nor the life try to impose on others what they believe to be the way. But these are only words that have no connection with real life or a real way. *When we understand and practice deeply the life and teachings*

of Buddha or the life and teachings of Jesus, we penetrate the door and enter the abode of the living Buddha and the living Christ, and life eternal presents itself to us.[99]

Cessation of unease comes as people follow the Eightfold Path, which is also known as the dharma wheel. Portrayed in Buddhist art, it looks, to Western eyes, something like an eight-spoked ship's wheel. It's a way to steer through the harmful breakers of life.

Peace Within: Right Meditation

In our fast-paced world, we are all too familiar with the tyranny of the urgent. "Hurry is not of the devil, it is the devil," is a saying often attributed to Carl Jung. Whether the famous psychoanalyst actually said it or not, modern research has found that the constant pressure to get things done *now* leads to a state of continuous stress, our bodies constantly pumping chemicals that wear away at our bodies and minds. Fortunately, meditation can bring relief.

Meditation is the last spoke of the Buddha's dharma wheel, but the last is by no means the least. Meditation provides physical and emotional relief, not to mention even greater benefits, for "in meditation we enter into . . . the very act of enlightenment."[100] This priority of meditative practices is not unique to Buddhism; we saw it in the royal yoga path in Hinduism, and in the next chapter, we shall see it is the most effective route to mastery in Taoism. It is also a (sometimes forgotten) vital element in Jewish and Christian wisdom traditions. The first Psalm describes a godly person as a frequent meditator, and Psalm 46 calls to the seeker of Divine intimacy: "Be still, and know that I am God."

Contemplative prayer is the practice of stillness while focusing our awareness on God's Presence: It is "hanging out" with God in silence, not even talking with our thoughts. The author of Psalm 131:2 (which some scholars think may have been a woman[101]) says, in effect, to God: "I'm quieted in your presence. Like a sleepy child resting on her mother's lap, my soul is content in you." Do you remember the good feeling of snuggling up with a parent when you were little? (Or as a parent or grandparent, snuggling with a little one?) Isn't it delightful to think of having that same experience in wordless prayer?

Contemplative prayer was also an important element in Celtic Christianity. Although there is scant information on the "how to" of ancient Celtic contemplative practices, we do know that both Pagan and early Christian Celts made use of stone "sweating houses," heated by peat fires. According to Celtic historian Peter Berresford Ellis, the person undergoing this process "was encouraged to meditate (*dercad*) to achieve a state of peace (*sitcháin*). This process has been found in many cultures in the world, such as among the Native American peoples, and has the same religious connotations as in the Celtic world."[102] Irish monks also practiced a contemplative prayer called *rinnfheitheamh.*

According to contemplative teacher Carl McColman, "*Rinn* means a 'point' or 'tip,' as in the sharp point of a sword. *Fheitheamh* means 'waiting.'" This form of prayer "acknowledges that 'edge' place in our hearts where time meets eternity, where words fade into silence, and where heaven silently gazes into the turmoil of earthly life."[103]

We know Celtic Christians followed the practices of the Egyptian saints, whom they admired deeply. The Desert Mothers and Fathers sought to diminish their egos—their selfish and false sense of self—in order to be absorbed into Divine Presence. One of the Desert Fathers, Evagrius of Pontus, who was an influential fourth-century Christian theologian and a master of silent prayer, taught: "Prayer is the suppression of every concept. Blessed is the mind which has acquired total absence of form at the moment of prayer."[104] Another desert master, Blessed Isaac described "perfection of heart" as "total and uninterrupted dedication to prayer," in which the person praying will "strive for unstirring calm of mind and for never-ended purity."[105] In modern times, Cistercian Father Thomas Keating encapsulated the wisdom of these Desert Mothers and Fathers in a technique he called Centering Prayer, today the most popular form of Christian contemplative prayer.[106]

The Star Wars universe presents a good illustration of how contemplative practices can aid us. In *The Phantom Menace*, Qui Gon Jinn (Luke's Jedi mentor) is in a life-and-death lightsaber duel with the demonic-looking Darth Maul. The combatants briefly separate, and a forcefield pops up between them, separating the two duelists. Darth Maul paces like a caged animal, driven by his restless anger—but Qui Gon settles into a classic meditation pose, his face serene. After a few moments, the force field disappears, and the Jedi is back on his feet in an instant, mentally refocused. In the same way, even amid a crisis, we too can mentally access the inner calm that comes from the daily practice of meditation.

Buddhist master Thich Nhat Hanh offers this description of the peaceful fruits of meditation:

> We often think of peace as the absence of war, that if powerful countries would reduce their weapon arsenals, we could have peace. But if we look deeply into the weapons, we see our own minds—our own prejudices, fears and ignorance. Even if we transport all the bombs to the moon, the roots of war and the roots of bombs are still there, in our hearts and

minds, and sooner or later we will make new bombs. To work for peace is to uproot war from ourselves and from the hearts of men and women.[107]

Peace Without: Right Actions

The first time I saw the image I wondered if it was photoshopped: the Dalai Lama, with his familiar broad smile and saffron garb, was holding a large St. Brigid's cross. It turns out His Holiness came to Kildare, Ireland, at the invitation of the Brigidine Sisters, who serve at the site of the saint's ancient monastery.[108] He recognized that he and this medieval Irish abbess share a common commitment to peace.

Domestic strife between clans was common in Brigid's time, and she often intervened to bring healing and reconciliation between rival factions. There's a famous story about Brigid's peacemaking way. When she was a young woman, Brigid's father attempted to sell her to the King of Leinster as his bride. While the men haggled over the bride price, Brigid stood waiting in her father's chariot. A leper approached asking for alms. Seeing her father's bejeweled heirloom sword and perceiving that the impoverished man was Christ appearing as "the least of these, my brethren, hungry" (Matthew

25), Brigid handed the man her father's sword. When the king and her father returned, they were both flabbergasted by Brigid's action. The king immediately called off the marriage, leaving Brigid free to pursue her spiritual calling as an independent woman. She had transformed an instrument of death into a source of life—a reminder of the Bible's call to turn swords into plowshares. Brigid and the abbesses who followed her were so active and effective in peacemaking that they were known as "women who turn back the streams of war."[109]

Brigid's and the Dalai Lama's commitments to peace originate in their religions, for both Jesus and Buddha commanded nonviolence. Jesus told his disciples, "If anyone strikes you on the cheek, offer the other also" (Luke 6:29), and the Buddha's fourth dharma principle—"right action"—includes the injunction not to destroy life.

Christ's first followers took literally his call to "love your enemies" and "put down your sword." They refused military service and guard duty because these professions required the use of lethal force. In the second century, Church Father Tertullian wrote, "If we are enjoined, then, to love our enemies . . . whom have we to hate? . . . Who can suffer injury at our hands?"[110]

Origen, Tertullian's contemporary, stated that "the taking of human life in any form at all" is incompatible with following Christ.[111] No early-Christian theologian approved of using lethal force—for either warfare or the enforcement of the law—before the Emperor Constantine promoted Christianity in the early fourth century.[112]

On October 28, 312, however, the Christian faith was severed from nonviolence with the first action of Christian nationalism. Two would-be Roman emperors, brothers Constantine and Maxentius, sent their armies into gory combat for control of their father's Imperial throne. Maxentius' army was annihilated, the Tiber flowed red with blood, and when the fog of war lifted Constantine proudly carried his brother's head into the city on a spike. That might not seem like an entirely Christ-like thing to do, but the newly victorious emperor made clear that he had won the battle at Christ's behest.

Before the battle Constantine claimed to have a vision of the cross accompanied by the words, "By this sign you shall conquer." He ordered his legionnaires to paint their shields with the symbol of the "Chi-Rho" (the first two Greek letters of the name *Christ*). After the carnage, the triumphant new emperor "believed that he had secured imperial power through the assistance of Jesus Christ."[113]

Even after this happened, many Christian leaders still insisted on pacifism. *The Canons of Hippolytus*, a list of thirty-eight decrees for Christian churches written in the mid-fourth century by Hippolytus, High Bishop of Rome, states "A soldier of civil authority must be taught not to kill men and to refuse to do so if he is commanded."[114] I can't help but wonder how the history of Christianity might differ if it had not been weaponized by the Roman Empire? Perhaps Christianity's long story might have been more akin to that of Buddhism.

Martin of Tours, who shaped the monasteries and practices of Celtic Christianity, followed the early Jesus tradition of love of enemy. Before Martin's conversion, the Roman army had conscripted him into service at the age of fifteen, and he had risen through the ranks. Then, when he was forty, he had a spiritual encounter with Jesus. On the eve of his next battle, Martin told the Emperor Julian, "Hitherto I have served you as a soldier; let me now serve Christ. . . . I am a soldier of Christ and it is not lawful for me to fight."[115] Martin was dismissed from military service, leading to his extraordinary influence as a hermit and later the founder of monasteries.

Christians today are divided over the morality of using lethal force for self-defense, policing, or national defense. Many Christians follow the just-war theory formulated by Augustine of Hippo, who argued that violence is moral if it prevents greater violence from spreading. Christian denominations such as the Amish, Mennonites, and Quakers remain committed to pacifism. Whatever their stance on the proper ethical use of force, Christ-followers have done little in the modern age to prevent violence within their societies or between nations. The peaceful conduct of the Buddha's followers throughout history should serve to remind Christians of Jesus' desire for peace.

Helpers: Kuan Yin and Brigid, Saints of Compassion

Two men, Buddha and Jesus, gave rise to the religions named after them, and in both traditions female exemplars soon rose to prominence beside these male founders. Wherever Buddhism has flourished, the Boddhisatva Kuan Yin has vied for loyalty alongside the Buddha, just as Mary the mother of Christ has been an icon of veneration beside her Son. And in Celtic spirituality,

Brigid of Kildare attained such status that she is often referred to as "Mary of the Gaels." Kuan Yin and Brigid seem to have similar pacifying roles in their respective religious traditions. I think of them as Asian and Celtic sisters for peace.

In the Buddhist tradition, Kuan Yin is a bodhi-sattva, a being who has escaped the delusions of this life and entered nirvana—but refuses to escape the suffering world and instead helps mortals find enlightenment. Bodhisattvas are similar to Christian saints.

Kuan Yin is a title rather than a name; it means, "One Who Hears the Cries of the Whole World." As the bodhisattva of compassion, Kuan Yin stands ready to aid humans whenever they need strength to forgive someone who has wronged them, love their enemy, or push through past hurts in order to heal. In this, she is much like Saint Brigid.

When we are tempted to violence, invoking the help of a female bodhisattva or saint can bring calm and a renewed commitment to compassion. The power of departed saints to assist in the spiritual struggles of the living may seem alien to readers reared in Protestantism; both conservative and liberal Protestants eschew the influence of the departed. For those open to widening their understanding of an invisible dimension, however, consider that Christ says his Divine Abba "is not the God of the dead but of the living," referring to the con-tinuing lives of Abraham, Isaac, and Jacob beyond the earthly pale (Mark 12:27). In the Book of Revelation, in John's vision of "the souls of those who have been slaughtered," he indicated that the departed are aware of events that unfold on earth and they request God to redress earthly wrongs (Revelation 6:9). I once heard a very conservative Calvinist Protestant theologian—using that verse—assured a congregation that their recently deceased minister still saw them from heaven, cared about their needs, and prayed for them.

How far of a stretch is it to reach from the scriptural passages above and expand to the idea of praying *with* (not *to*) those who have gone ahead of us to Glory? Perhaps you have known a prayer partner who faithfully intercedes for you through thick and thin. If they passed on into eternity, must you cease asking them to pray for you? Christ says they still live; you just can't see them. Why not ask for their help in prayer? It is not hard for me to imagine my mother in heaven praying for me; after all, I know she still loves me and desires my good. Besides my mom, might not Blessed Brigid, my spiritual ancestress in Christ, pray for me also?

If this has begun to sound too woo-woo to you, you may receive help from a different perspective on departed saints. Who can deny the power of great figures—historical, literary, and mythic—to inspire us, empowering us by their example to do great deeds? Even beloved Star Wars characters or Marvel Comics superheroes can serve us in this way; Captain Jean Luc Picard of Star Trek fame is one of my personal role models and heroes. If fictional creations can move people, how much more can the great exemplars of spiritual traditions inspire our courageous deeds?

Consider how you feel after saying this traditional prayer to Brigid:

Brigid, you were a woman of peace,
you brought harmony where there was conflict.
You brought light into the darkness.
You brought hope to the downcast.
May the mantle of your peace
cover those who are troubled and anxious,
and may peace be firmly rooted in
our hearts and in our world.
Inspire us to act justly and reverence
all that God has made.
Brigid, you were a voice for the wounded and the weary.
Strengthen what is weak within us.
Calm us into quietness that heals and listens.
May we grow each day into greater
wholeness in mind, body, and spirit.
Amen

Now, read this prayer to Kuan Yin, written by an American Buddhist teacher, Bhikshuni Thubten Chodron:

> *Just as when frightened, children seek protection and refuge in their mother's comforting arms, so do we children of the Dharma seek protection and refuge in you when saddened and horrified by the suffering of this world. . . . In tragedy may we turn to wisdom and compassion and be comforted by its protective embrace. Seeing that all beings seek only happiness and never misery, may we abandon despair, anger, and blame. May all those who suffer from loss and grief, from horror and outrage, become fountains of wisdom and compassion flowing out to the world and healing beings' pain. . . . By holding ourselves and others responsible for our misdeeds, may we too hear the cries of the world. And with compassion may all of us overcome the self-centered attitude and create a better world—one in which everyone seeks to benefit each other.*[116]

In this world's struggle for peace, we are not alone. We have heavenly companions who work alongside us.

Forgiveness and Justice: Twin Pillars of Peace

Patrick of Ireland is an example of the forgiveness required to make peace—and yet he also reminds us that true peace cannot be forged until injustices are redressed.

Sometime around the year 400, Patrick was a teenager going about his daily life on the west coast of Britain when Irish pirates landed, captured him, and carried him away. During the next six years, as he labored and suffered as a slave, he turned to God. He became accustomed to hearing God's voice, so when the Word urged, "Get up and run to the opposite coast, there's a boat there that will take you home," he did so, regardless of the harsh punishment threatened for runaway slaves. When he reentered his parents' home, his family must have thought it was a miracle.

He had returned different from when he left; the experience had transformed him. This became evident when an angel from Ireland appeared in his night dreams, insisting that he return to share the love of Christ with his former captors and tormentors. Patrick underwent proper training for ordination in the church and then departed for Ireland.

To call this courageous is an understatement. He risked death and torture, yet he went unarmed. Some say he came equipped with gifts for the chieftains, some say he brought a brewer to share the gift of ale, and others claim his greatest asset was a fine voice and gift for verse. Whatever he had, it worked. By the time he died, decades later, the northern half of Ireland sang praises to Christ.

Patrick came to Ireland as a living model of the Christ he proclaimed. He came in the power of servanthood, self-denying love, and forgiveness for those who had wronged him. Patrick of Ireland is an inspiring historical model of Christian forgiveness, but he also serves as an example of a contemporary slogan: "No justice, no peace."

When the soldiers of a British king raided Ireland's shores and enslaved Irish women and men, Patrick was filled with righteous anger. He knew from his own experience the pain of those who were enslaved and taken to a foreign land. The raiding king, Coroticus, claimed to be a Christian. Patrick wrote him an open letter declaring that slaving and raiding were offenses against God, that the king's piety—rather than saving him—would condemn him.

In our world today, victims of racism, homophobia, sexism, and other prejudices are resisting those in more-privileged positions, who often tell them, "Just forgive and get over it." Peace in the real world can only happen, however, after perpetrators repent of their sins against others. "Righteousness and peace will kiss each other," declares the psalmist (85:10). Demanding forgiveness from people still suffering mistreatment is not righteousness but just another form of abuse, one that lays still more injustice on a pile of unaddressed wrongs. This form of injustice occurs when whites complain about "violence" in Black Lives Matter protests, men complain about "angry women," or straight folks ask why LGBTQ+ neighbors "have to make a show" of their queerness. Real peace must be accompanied by justice.

Consider the strident voice of Jesus addressing religious leaders who abused their dynamics of power: "They tie up heavy burdens, hard to bear, and lay them on the shoulders of others, but they themselves are unwilling to lift a finger to move them" (Matthew 23:4). "Woe to you. . . . For you are like whitewashed tombs, which on the outside look beautiful but on the inside are full of . . . all kinds of uncleanness. So you also on the outside look righteous to others, but inside you are full of hypocrisy and lawlessness" (Matthew 23:27–28).

Buddha, like Christ, taught the need for justice to go with compassion. In May of 2015, prominent Buddhist teachers signed a document titled, "Statement on Racism from Buddhist Teachers & Leaders in the United States." They affirmed that "we can't separate our personal healing and transformation from that of our larger society. The historic and continued suffering of people of color in this country—of African Americans, Native Americans, Latinos, Asian Americans and others—is our collective suffering. The harm caused daily is our collective responsibility." They went on to say:

> Since their inception, Buddhist teachings and practices have been explicitly devoted to liberation. In his time the Buddha was a revolutionary voice against racism and the caste system: "Not by caste, race, or creed, or birth is one noble, but by heart alone is one a noble being." The Buddhist trainings in mindfulness, wisdom and compassion, create the grounds for wise speech and wise action. These teachings and practices free our hearts from greed, prejudice and hate and serve an essential role in societal healing, and in the awakening of all.[117]

The call to justice with reconciliation is a great challenge but not as immense as the suffering that happens if people of faith do not pursue it. Buddhists can call upon the strength of their Buddha-nature; Christians can call upon Christ's indwelling Spirit. Some will feel more comfortable asking aid from Kuan Yin, Mary, or Brigid. The forces of injustice seem daunting—but how can they possibly stand against the overwhelming strength of such love?

DISCUSSION QUESTIONS

The title *Buddha* means "Awakened One." Is there a time you experienced a substantial "awakening"?

What attachments rob you of joy?

How can you love people, places, and things without being attached to them?

SPIRITUAL PRACTICES

Read through the Sermon on the Mount (Matthew 5-7) and compare it with the Eightfold Path.

Look online for a guided Loving Kindness (Metta) meditation. This is a powerful tool for unleashing compassion. Tara Brach has a good video of this practice.

Practice mindfulness. Observe the present moment as it is. Don't struggle to achieve some great life-changing epiphany. The goal is simple: simply pay attention to the present moment, without judgment. Again, look online for guided mindfulness meditations (for example, videos by Daily Calm).

Interdependence is an important Buddhist concept. Pick an object—human-made or natural, large or small, ordinary or extraordinary. Then think about the forces that made it, sustain it, use it, etc. Think of as many connections as you can with one object.

Do you think of the saints as still-living beings? Consider how the great Celtic saints such as Aidan, Hilda, Cuthbert, Brigid, and Patrick, as well as Buddhist heavenly guides, might help you on your journey to illumined living.

What things have you unwittingly invested with power to make you happy or sad by their presence or absence? Remember, you can (and should) love people and enjoy things—and that will be even more rewarding on a nonattachment basis. Spend time considering that your happiness comes from within. Say to each attachment, "I have cheated myself by believing that without you I cannot be happy."

Buddhist kindness meditation is essentially a practice of blessing. Saunter about and silently say a blessing for every person, creature, and object that meets your gaze.

Practice reciting a mantra. Either walking or sitting, indoors or outdoors, repeat a phrase that leads to your divine center. The most common Buddhist phrase is, "Om mani padme hum" (Om, Jewel, Lotus, yes!), and the most common Christian mantra is the Jesus Prayer: "Lord Jesus Christ, Son of God, Have mercy on me, a sinner."

Work for justice. Climate injustice, racism, violence—what issue calls you? Sometimes we avoid involvement because we don't want to be overwhelmed by emotions of fear, depression, or anger. Remember, with a nondual perspective you can grieve the realities of brokenness and evil while simultaneously rejoicing in the Divine Presence that underlies the realm of the senses. Find a way to work for change that fits your particular gifts and resources.

CELTIC SPIRITUALITY
AND TAOISM

Going with the Flow

Luke Skywalker: Breathe. Just breathe.
Reach out with your feelings. What do you see?

Rey: The island. Life. Death and decay,
that feeds new life. Warmth. Cold. Peace. Violence.

Luke: And between it all?

Rey: Balance. An energy. A Force.

Luke: And inside you?

Rey: Inside me, that same Force.

—The Last Jedi [118]

I live in rural America, where folks are prone to speaking bluntly yet with humor. A common saying around here is, "Life is hard, but it's harder when you're stupid." I have to confess, sometimes I do things that fall in the category of "stupid."

My wife has a nickname for me: absent-minded professor. I swear, that's not true. I'm not currently employed by any college, so only the first two words are accurate. I'm not extraordinarily tall, and yet I have managed over the years to achieve a solid record of banging my head into doorway casings; I once even concussed myself entering a Scottish castle. The more intensely I'm thinking about something other than my surroundings, the more likely I am to do something silly like this.

Unmindful actions can have painful consequences. By contrast, there's a delightful description of the Celtic saints: "The saints were never hurried; they did comparatively few things . . . Yet they always seemed to hit the mark; every bit of their life told." [119]

Taoists make a tantalizing claim that we can live in the same satisfying manner as those saints. They call this exquisite way of living *wu wei* (pronounced like "woo way"). Master teacher Qiguang Zhao explains: "The goal of Wu Wei is to achieve a state of spontaneous alignment with the Tao, and, as a result, obtain a perfect form of supple and invisible power."[120] This is not the "power" of worldly success but the joy of living in harmony with the elemental and spiritual forces of the universe. Taoism claims that wu wei can be learned—and after devoting myself to this practice, I do have fewer bumps on my forehead!

The Tao

Some years ago, as I sat talking with a Taoist master trained in the intricacies of a 1,500-year-old mystic tradition, I posed this question: "What is the Tao? How do you grasp it?"

"You know Star Wars?" he asked. "The Force?"

I nodded.

"That is the Tao," he said.

The best-known saying about the Tao comes from the first words of the Tao Te Ching: "The Tao that can be described in words is not the true Tao: The name that can be named is not the true Name."[121] According to legend, the enlightened master Lao Tzu, who wrote this spiritual classic sometime around 500 BCE, had declared his intention to flee humankind and live alone in the wilderness. People begged him not to leave without imparting his knowledge, so he spent a night scribbling down his philosophy. The next morning, he tossed it over his shoulder as he walked away. Did Lao Tzu live in caves thereafter? Did he ascend to higher realms as an immortal? No one knows. After imparting his wisdom in written form, he disappeared forever from recorded history.

Lao Tzu's emphasis on the mysterious nature of the Divine accords with the Lakota Nation's understanding of the sacred as Wakan Tanka, which translates as "Great Mystery." Likewise, medieval mystics insist God is above human understanding.

While Lao Tzu begins his teachings by saying, "I can't really explain the Tao," by the twenty-fifth chapter of the Tao Te Ching, he tries to do just that (a good example of nondual thinking!):

> *There was something formless and perfect*
> *before the universe was born.*
> *It is serene.*
> *Empty.*
> *Solitary.*
> *Unchanging.*
> *Infinite.*
> *Eternally present.*
> *It is the Mother of the universe.*
> *For lack of a better name, I call it the Tao.*[122]

As Master Yoda, in *The Empire Strikes Back*, says about the Force, "Its energy surrounds us and binds us . . . You must feel the Force around you; here, between you, me, the tree, the rock, everywhere, yes."[123] This sounds akin to Saint Ninian's ancient Celtic catechism, which says that the goal of wisdom is to "perceive the eternal Word of God reflected in every plant and insect, every bird and animal, and every man and woman."[124]

Insights from today's scientists and theologians also conjoin with the ancient Chinese understanding of the Tao. Ilia Delio, a theologian specializing in evolution, neuroscience, and quantum physics, speculates that "consciousness may be part of inanimate matter from the Big Bang cosmos onward,"[125] while Franciscan priest Richard Rohr asserts that "everything visible, without exception, is the outpouring of God. . . . 'Christ' is a word for the Primordial Template (Logos) through whom 'All things came into being' (John 1:3)."[126] Meanwhile, centuries earlier, Lao Tzu wrote: "The great Tao flows everywhere. All things are born from it. . . . It pours itself into its work. . . . It nourishes infinite worlds."

The obvious question: "Is the Tao God?" Interspiritual theologian John Mabry wisely answers, "Yes and no." He says, "*The Tao is God as nature sees God. . . . The* sparrow does not perceive God as a personality but as the very web of being in which it moves and it consists. The Taoist follows the example of the animals and the Earth herself and perceives God in the same way."[127]

Taoist writings also highlight the importance of the Divine Feminine. The Tao is "the womb giving birth to all of being" and "an origin which we may regard as the mother of the universe."[128] While Western Christianity has obscured a feminine Divinity, theologian Lynne Bundesen describes her lifelong journey of Bible study, during which, she says:

> I've discovered feminine-gendered nouns and pronouns in the original languages, which had been hidden by both the English translations and my own assumption that the biblical God was male. I found verbs applied to God's action that could only describe women's experiences—and yet centuries of male translators had minimized, obscured, or obliterated that meaning. Finding these clues has been a lifelong treasure hunt, filled with the thrill of discovery. Rising above that, however, and even more important to me, was the consistent conviction that the biblical writers do describe a Divine Feminine Spirit who is present and transformative.[129]

Bundesen goes on to cite many specific examples throughout the Bible. Like the Tao, the Judeo-Christian scriptures speak of the Divine womb that gives birth to all Creation. Underlying all events and all objects in the universe flows the mothering current of the Tao.

Wu Wei—or Life in the Spirit

Wu wei is the Taoist art of immersing our lives in the Tao's current. The concept became personal and vital for me during a weeklong retreat with Scottish abbess Fionn Tulach, who was teaching the ways of the Ceili De (an ancient and continuing Celtic monastic order). On the second day of the retreat, when Fionn wrote on a whiteboard the word *Coinneach*, I at once perked up; my given name, Kenneth, is *Coinneach* in Scots Gaelic—and now Fionn said the word means "to go with the Divine flow." At lunchtime, I approached Fionn, told her my name, and asked if she could say more about the meaning. The abbess replied, "If you happen to know about Taoism, then *coinneach* is wu wei." That conversation set me on a challenging but rewarding journey of trying to live into the deeper meaning of my name.

My namesake, Saint Coinneach, was a sixth-century Irishman, a close friend of the more famous Saint Columba. The son of a bard, Coinneach was schooled in Wales and then set up a monastery at Kilkenny in Ireland. One fun bit of trivia from his medieval hagiography is that a dragon bit off his toe[130]—but more significant than the missing toe is a saying associated with him: "I hear the voice of the waves chanting and calling to us: what are they singing?"[131] That expression accords with the Taoist understanding that "water is the essence of Wu Wei."[132]

Imagine reality as a vast, fast-moving river with patches of fierce whitewater. This river is the manifestation of the Tao, and we humans are all trying to navigate the river. Those of us who live the least skillful lives—impeded by our egos, selfishness, anger, or hatred—spend much of our lives going against the current; hence, we are constantly frustrated and worn down. Others of us, blinded by ignorance or pride, refuse to accept the realities of the river, and the flow tumbles us against the boulders, so that we suffer badly. But some of us, who are focused on the flow of the Tao, are like skilled river-runners in kayaks, skimming along atop the whitewater, flowing with the current. Unlike the others, who are struggling against the great force of the water, these experts only need to make slight efforts to propel themselves forward. A few quick thrusts with their paddles will allow them to zip past a log in the river or steer them into alignment with the fastest channel. This is encapsulated in a Chinese proverb: "Push the boat with the current."[133]

Wu wei is the art of flowing with the current of the Tao. Remember, the Tao in its transcendent nature is unseen, yet it is always manifest in the natural world. As

Celtic Christians saw Christ in wind, wave, oak, and stag, so the Tao is tangible in natural forces. To master wu wei, we need to live in connection and harmony with Nature.

The seventeenth-century Welsh cleric Thomas Traherne seems like a master of wu wei (although it is unlikely he ever heard of Taoism); in reality, he is a good example of the ongoing influence of Celtic spirituality. Although Traherne lived in times of personal, professional, and societal upheaval, he found abiding joyfulness during his time outdoors. He describes the life-giving flow he experienced in the natural world:

> *A Native Health and Innocence*
> *Within my Bones did grow,*
> *And while my God did all his Glories shew,*
> *I felt a vigour in my Sence*
> *That was all Spirit.*
> *I within did flow*
> *With Seas of Life, like Wine;*
> *I nothing in the World did know,*
> *But 'twas Divine.*[134]

To get a feel for the flow of the Tao, we too can observe the cycles of Nature, marking as the ancient Celts did the changes of daytime and nighttime, the shifting patterns of animal and plant life, and the great cosmic calendar cycles set by the Sun and Moon. The connection between humans, the Tao, and the larger sphere of Creation flows back and forth. Just as the natural world affects our moods, our inner state can affect the larger world.

Carl Jung liked to tell a story he'd heard from one of his friends who had lived in China:

> There was a great drought where [Jung's friend lived]; for months there had not been a drop of rain and the situation became catastrophic. The Catholics made processions, the Protestants made prayers, and the Chinese burned joss-sticks and shot off guns to frighten away the demons of the drought, but with no result.
>
> Finally . . . from another province a dried up old man appeared. The only thing he asked for was a quiet little house somewhere, and there he locked himself in for three days.
>
> On the fourth day the clouds gathered and there was a great snow-storm at the time of the year when no snow was expected, an unusual amount, and the town was so full

of rumours about the wonderful rain-maker that [Jung's friend] went to ask the man how he did it.

In true European fashion he said: 'They call you the rain-maker; will you tell me how you made the snow?'

And the rain-maker said: "I did not make the snow; I am not responsible."

"But what have you done these three days?"

". . . I come from another country where things are in order. Here they are out of order, therefore, the whole country is not in Tao, and I also am not in the natural order of things because I am in a disordered country. So, I had to wait three days until I was back in Tao and then naturally the rain came."[135]

The rain-maker's presence was enough to restore order to a disordered corner of the universe. Modern physics indicates that whenever we observe something, we influence it. Our inner awareness touches and shapes the world around us.

Wu wei also means listening to the needs of our body with its built-in desires for exercise, food, and rest.

We tend to push our bodies according to the imposed dictates of our schedules, and in the process, we get too little exercise, skip meals, and stare for hours at screens. If we learned to live in harmony with the flow of our own bodies, we'd be far healthier.

The flow of the Tao may have little to do with the goals and deadlines that lash us forward each day. Nature is not a treadmill: It is free and spontaneous. Birds do not give themselves ulcers thinking about which branch to alight on or what berry to pick. Fish do not get heart attacks swimming until they die exhausted. The wind, as Jesus says, "blows where it chooses" (John 3:8). A person who has mastered wu wei conducts herself more like a serendipitous wind or free-flying sparrow than as someone beholden to another's schedule.

The Way to Wu Wei— or Openness to the Spirit

Wu wei is openness to "what is," acceptance of whatever the flow delivers to our lives. As Lao Tzu wrote: "The Master gives himself up to whatever the moment brings. . . . He doesn't think about his actions; they flow from the core of his being. He holds nothing back from life."

This is also what Jesus taught when he urged all who follow his path:

> "Therefore I tell you, do not worry about your life, what you will eat or what you will drink, or about your body, what you will wear. Is not life more than food and the body more than clothing? Look at the birds of the air: they neither sow nor reap nor gather into barns, and yet your heavenly Father feeds them. Are you not of more value than they? And which of you by worrying can add a single hour to your span of life? And why do you worry about clothing? Consider the lilies of the field, how they grow; they neither toil nor spin, yet I tell you, even Solomon in all his glory was not clothed like one of these. But if God so clothes the grass of the field, which is alive today and tomorrow is thrown into the oven, will he not much more clothe you—you of little faith? Therefore do not worry, saying, 'What will we eat?' or 'What will we drink?' or 'What will we wear?' For . . . indeed your heavenly Father knows that you need all these things. But seek first the kingdom of God and

his righteousness, and all these things will be given to you as well. So do not worry about tomorrow, for tomorrow will bring worries of its own. Today's trouble is enough for today. (Matthew 6:25–34)

The Sufi poet Rumi describes this openness to whatever the moment brings, recommending that we think of our lives as "guest houses," where

every morning a new guest arrives.
Sometimes it's joy, other days it's sadness.
Some days irritation and aggravation;
other days a new insight arrives like an unexpected visitor.
Help me, Divine Lover,
to welcome each and every guest.
Even if a crowd of sorrows
comes pushing through my door
and robs all my furniture,
give me strength to treat them like honored guests.[136]

The Chinese philosophy of wu wei may be a fresh way for Christians to understand one of the central ideas of their faith: the leading of the Holy Spirit. Jesus was like the perfect Taoist master, in that his life was entirely led and filled by Spirit (Luke 4:14,16).

Like Wu Wei, life in the Spirit is likened to following the flow of water; in John's Gospel, Jesus declares, "Out of the believer's heart shall flow rivers of living water," and the narrator comments, "Now he said this about the Spirit, which believers in him were to receive" (John 14:38–39).

The effects of the Spirit—like those of the Tao—are an instinctively virtuous life. Modern Celtic author and spiritual leader Ray Simpson writes: "Sometimes we experience the Spirit as a gentle breeze: inspiring us to grow in goodness, refreshing us, giving us peace. At other times we experience the Spirit as a wild wind, blowing us out of our safe little boxes. This Way of Life calls us to let the Spirit blow us anywhere."[137]

The apostle Paul told Christians to "walk by the Spirit" and "If we live by the Spirit, let us also be guided by the Spirit," for "the fruit of the Spirit is love, joy, peace, patience, kindness, generosity, faithfulness, gentleness, and self-control" (Galatians 5:22, 25). If "guided by the Spirit" does not strike us as following wu wei, perhaps it is because many Christians have forgotten the efficacy, spontaneity, and joy of being Spirit-led.

Some of today's Celtic Christians have adopted the wild goose as a symbol of the Holy Spirit, rather than the more placid dove, because the wild goose is a reminder of the Spirit's great power and untamed ways. Openness to the Spirit involves excitement and great possibility. She offers enticing possibilities of transformation—and yet there is also an element of risk when we open ourselves to her impulses. Women and men taking membership vows in the Celtic community of Aidan and Hilda are told, "You have heard the call of the wild goose, the untamable Spirit of God: Be ready for the Spirit to lead you into the wild, windy, or well-worn places of wonder and welcome."

These vows are also known as "the taking of the coracle," a phrase describing a spirit-guided life that recalls how early Celtic Christians "sometimes voyaged in coracles without oars and let God's winds take them wherever God willed."[138] Sounds a lot like the Taoist phrase "push the boat with the current," doesn't it?

The Practice of Wu Wei

While it is perfectly natural, a life of wu wei does not necessarily come to us naturally. I was raised to be self-controlled, goal-focused, and always rational—which has meant I have had to struggle to unlearn habits that hinder openness to the Spirit. I have only begun in some small measure to live up to my name, to let go and enter the Divine flow.

Spiritual practices can retrain our minds and souls to feel the flow of Divinity and to flow along with it. One of the simplest is to do things aimlessly or playfully. The great spiritual teacher Alan Watts reminds us:

> Children (and adults who have their wisdom) are usually the most happy when they are doing things that have no particular purpose—making up lunatic stories with friends, walking aimlessly through fields and hitting at old stumps with a stick . . . the contemplative happiness of these things belongs to that childlike wisdom which must be learned again before one may enter the kingdom of heaven."[139]

A related and overlapping practice is letting go of outcomes. From our first day of kindergarten to our very last day in the workplace, many of us are hell-bent on success. If we don't produce a tangible product, fail to achieve quota benchmarks, or lack substantial financial profits as a result of our actions, we feel as though we are "wasting time." The Taoist adept, however, who follows the course of Nature, knows that "in your life you can be successful or unsuccessful: it doesn't matter, as long as you flow with the time."[140]

To live by the Spirit or flow in the Tao, we must let go of our need for others' approval. Lao Tzu offers a lovely description of how letting go of self-ambition brings real peace: "Care about people's approval and you will be their prisoner. Do your work, then step back. This is the only path to serenity."

To live by the Spirit, in the flow of the Tao, we must also let go of our egos, the false selves we hide behind, those illusory self-sufficient entities. As Lao Tzu explains: "Hope and fear are both phantoms that arise from thinking of the self. When we don't see the self as self, what do we have to fear?" The Bible's Book of Proverbs also contrasts the ego-directed life with Spirit-guided life:

Trust in the Life-Giver with all your being,
and do not rely on your own insight or desires.
In all your ways acknowledge the Living One,
who will guide you along straight paths.
(Proverbs 3:5, 6, my paraphrase)

Lao Tzu offers explains that clinging to a false self does not achieve success, while only by letting go of self-ambition do we find real peace:

Fill your bowl to the brim
and it will spill.
Keep sharpening your knife
and it will blunt.
Chase after money and security
and your heart will never unclench.
Care about people's approval
and you will be their prisoner.
Do your work, then step back.
The only path to serenity.

When we let go of ego, we stop taking things personally. We no longer preen ourselves over others' approval and compliments, nor do we torment ourselves with self-doubt if others criticize us or reject us. As Lao Tzu said, "When you are content to be simply yourself and don't compare or compete, everybody will respect you."

Walking by the Spirit—wu wei—also requires reliance on our faculties of intuition. Have you ever had a feeling that you should—or should not—do something? Maybe it was a nagging thought: *I should check in on so-and-so*—and then you discover the other person really needs to talk about an urgent concern. Or you think, *I should drive a different route this morning*, and that uncommon direction leads you to an unexpected opportunity. Taoist wisdom invites us to listen to our own inner voices, to trust our intuition as a personal connection with the Tao. The Tao moves in ways of utter selflessness, awareness of others, and looking for the common good. A person highly skilled in wu wei will also be a living illustration of the compassionate Christ Way. And this life will come naturally.

To those who master wu wei, many wise decisions come without thought. The Taoist Master doesn't have to stop mid-action and ponder: *What is the right thing for me to do in this situation?* By the time she pondered—and arrived at a decision—it would likely be too late; how much better to have set the habit of wu wei, going with the flow! Guided by Spirit-current, she can quickly and effectively do the right thing, naturally. Asian warriors explain intuitive guidance with the saying, "The sword swings itself," meaning you cannot survive battle if you have to consciously decide on each thrust or parry; the master swordsman has practiced so much he does the right thing intuitively, naturally.

One who flows with the Tao—with Spirit—will instinctively do the right thing. As Lao Tzu puts it, "Stop thinking and end your problems." Yet that is not the ultimate end of wu wei. As in all the perennial spirit of all faith traditions, the true goal of practice is union with the Divine. As Lao Tzu testified, "I am different from ordinary people. I drink from the Great Mother's breasts"—and the apostle Paul said, "It is no longer I who live, but it is Christ who lives in me" (Galatians 2:20).

Immɾɑmɑ

Ancient Celtic spirituality has legends that teach us about *coinneach*—going with the Divine flow—tales of *immrama*, supernaturally inspired voyages into the unknown. The most famous of these is the *Navigatio* of Saint Brendan, which was a medieval bestseller. The story tells how a sixth-century Irish abbot set forth with a small crew from Ireland's West Coast in a hide-covered sailboat into the Atlantic Ocean. On their voyage, they beheld wondrous sights, landed on strange shores, and—true to formula—reached "the Land of Promise" before eventually returning to Ireland.

This Irish tale makes me think of Qiguang Zhao's explanation of wu wei: "The great ocean sends us drifting like a raft, the running river sweeps us along like a reed. We do not tell the ocean to stop its tides, and we do not tell the river to flow slower. We just trust them to celebrate the existence of happiness and freedom. We let water carry us to a new adventure."[141]

May this lovely prayer, attributed to Brendan, help you to "go with the flow," experiencing the Divine Presence in each aspect of your life:

Help me to journey beyond the familiar
and into the unknown.
Give me the faith to leave old ways
and break fresh ground with You.
Christ of the mysteries, I trust You
to be stronger than each storm within me.
I will trust in the darkness and know
that my times, even now, are in Your hand.
Tune my spirit to the music of heaven,
and somehow, make my obedience count for You.

DISCUSSION QUESTIONS

How do you address the Divine in prayer? Do you think of God/Tao in masculine or feminine terms? How would changing that alter your relationship with the Divine?

In what natural objects or formations do you most easily glimpse the Spirit? In what plants, trees, or flowers? In what animals? In which humans?

When in life are you most comfortable going with the flow?

When in life are you most *un*comfortable going with the flow?

When in the past have you "let go" and trusted the Spirit? How did that turn out?

Where in life would you like to begin trusting Spirit more?

Picture yourself in the great river that is Divine Tao. Are you gasping against the current, sitting on the shore, or riding the waves smoothly?

What spiritual practices would be most helpful for you to grow in mastery of wu wei? In the past, how have you heard God's guiding word?

SPIRITUAL PRACTICES

Wu-Wei Walking

You can embark on this exercise from your own home or workplace, but it is more effective if you start out from an unfamiliar location. Then, as soon as you exit the building, try to intuit (rather than plan or think) where you are going. Let your feelings guide you. Do you feel drawn left or right? Does something grab your attention? Ask the Spirit to guide your steps and draw your attention to what She wants you to experience.

Walk in beauty. Go to a forest path or natural setting, a wild place that pleases you. What sights, objects, or natural features stir your senses? Focus on them. Be curious about why they draw you. What do they speak to you?

What do the waves chant? This saying of Saint Coinneach can be taken literally: Sit by an oceanside and listen to the surf or to a riverside with a strong current. Does the moving water tell you something? If you are journaling, let your hand flow across the page without stopping to consider or censure your words. Then consider Coinneach's words metaphorically: What are the "waves" lapping at your life? What are they saying to you?

Read (and reread) the Tao Te Ching. (I recommend Stephen Mitchell's translation.) What passages or thoughts strike you as similar to the wisdom of the Jewish and Christian scriptures? What passages of this classic Taoist work of literature speak to you most deeply?

Practice not doing. Leave your phone at home and go somewhere without it. Lie down on a beach. Watch the clouds drift overhead. Sit in a coffee shop and just sip coffee with no aim in mind. How does it feel? Why don't you do this more often?

Choose Your Own Immrama

And now I offer you the script for your own Immrama, an opportunity to shove off on an adventure, afloat on your own imagination. Along this voyage, I will ask you questions, and you may find it helpful to journal your answers.

A noisy rook roused you from sleep caw-ing loudly near your window at first light. Now, having stepped from bed, washed, and dressed, you step outside to stretch and feel the breeze. Wisps of morning fog curl slowly back and forth on the green grass that lies between your home and a beach. Beyond is the great ocean.

You walk toward the water, and coils of mist part to reveal a tall person clad in shimmer-ing white garments and rainbow-colored jewels. They smile, then call your name. "You must ride the wave path," they say, and they motion to a boat that's drifting close to the shore.

The boat has high curled prows and graceful lines that reflect the lapping waves. From the prow hangs a shield, and on that shield is your own heraldic crest, a unique design that captures your individual nature and strength.

What is the form on that crest? And how does it represent you? Ponder for a few moments.

You notice now that the beautiful stranger is holding out a gleaming object for you to take. "Take this," they say, "and keep it close to you on your voyage. It will empower you and guard you on the way."

What is this holy thing? What is the perfect protective talisman for your journey through life? Picture this sacred object in as much detail as you can. Consider finding a representative talisman (a stone, crystal, feather, or some other small object) to carry in your pocket as a reminder.

"Your vessel awaits," the extraordinary being tells you now. "It will carry you through any

peril and never succumb to any wave. Yet you lack instruction and a crew. Go from here and find the hermit—you know the one of which I speak—and ask that sage for a word before your journey. Then gather companions, the people who have upheld you through your earthly sojourn before now. They will be your crew."

Clutching the sacred object and filled with excitement, you leave the strange messenger and the ship behind you, hurrying past your home and up a long grassy hillside toward the forest above. You've spent many happy days in these woods, watching the birds, squirrels, and deer play, and you know the way to the hermit's hut. Although you don't ordinarily take this route—you know the recluse values privacy—you trust the stranger's instructions.

The hermit's hut is built into the side of a great oak, amazing in its girth. Moss has grown onto the hewn timbers of this holy person's home, so it almost seems as if tree and house are an organic one. You raise your hand to knock on the door, but as you hesitate, the hermit opens the portal.

"I've been expecting you," they say. "The one who calls you oceanward said you would come."

You nod, too overcome with wonder to speak.

"We need not tarry," says the wise one. "You are here for a word—which in fact is a warning: Wherever you journey, whatever port or strange isle you enter, you must always beware."

What is it that the hermit warns you of? What is the caution you must always be aware of? Sit until you have a clear understanding.

Dismissed by the sage, you set about to gather your crew. You will select from people you've known over the course of your life. Some are alive, others may already have passed from this life, but you can summon them from your memories and have them accompany you on this voyage. Some may live near you, others may be far away. You may have known them for a long time and on many occasions, or they may be someone who impacted you in a significant way though you otherwise hardly knew them.

Who will be your companions on this voyage? Take time to mentally choose your crew from your own family, friends, and meaningful acquaintances. You might want to also include characters from books or history, if these individuals have shaped you in some way.

The company gathered and your sacred object secured in a sturdy satchel, you head back to the sea The bright stranger smiles and stands beside the magical ship, their arm beckoning you to board with your crew. You wade through the shallow water and clamber aboard. As the stranger loosens the ropes that bind the vessel to its mooring, an enormous, feathered body bursts out of the ocean ahead of you—a gigantic swan with vast wings, long neck, bright eyes, and shining beak. One of your chosen companions lassos its neck, and the swan begins to swiftly pull your vessel seaward.

Behind you, you hear the stranger's voice from the rapidly receding shore: "Sail on, without fear! Follow the swan wherever she leads. Seek adventure with full delight! And

*do not turn back until your eyes behold that
which you most desire to see."*

What does the swan represent to you? Have you ever
sensed her presence in your life? What is it you most
desire to behold on this voyage?

*This is indeed a magical craft. Time and dis-
tance pass fly by such that you cannot tell
if hours or days have passed, nor can you
begin to guess how many leagues you have
traversed as you watch the sea spray off
the gigantic swan's back. You gaze at your
gathered companions and see they are also
entranced by this marvelous journey you
have all undertaken.*

*You hear and feel an enormous splash to one
side of your boat; a whale breaches the surface of the deep. As it soars into the air, water
cascading off its great back, time seems to
slow. The whale's eye meets yours—and then
it speaks to you! Its voice thunders in your
mind.*

What would a whale have to say to you? What unique
message does *this* whale bring to you?

And now the swan slows. You see a shore-line; a village; houses rising up just off the quay; sea birds with long, trailing feathers; and people standing on the beach to meet your boat. A little further inland are steps ascending an escarpment of bare rock, and atop that stands a castle. Its buttresses seem suspended in the air, and the windows dazzle your eyes with reflected light.

The ship bumps gently against a dock, and waiting hands secure its ropes. With warm and genuine smiles, people invite you to come ashore. "Welcome, we expected you!" they cry. "For a long time now, this place has awaited your coming."

What will you see when you climb the steps to the castle and the gates swing open? What awaits your coming?

From here on, this is entirely your own immrama. Journal the ongoing story of your adventure, using your imagination to reveal the deeper meanings of your life.

REFERENCE NOTES

Chapter 1: Strength of Oak, Beauty of Lotus

1.   Eden Phillpots, *A Shadow Passes* (London: Cecil Palmer & Hayward, 1918), 19.

2.   Joy Yates, "Zen and Now: Life Under Lockdown on Scotland's Holy Isle," *The Scotsman* (22 June 2020), https://www.scotsman.com/news/.

3.   Bruce Epperly, *Process Theology and Celtic Wisdom* (Gonzales, FL: Energion, 2021), 18.

4.   Martyn McLaughlin, "Holy Island Buddhists Fight Power Plant," *The Scotsman* (Sunday, 29 July 2012), https://www.scotsman.com/heritage-and-retro/.

5.   Nick Mayhew Smith, *Britain's Holiest Places: The All-New Guide to 500 Sacred Sites* (Bristol, UK: Lifestyle Press, 2011), 473.

6.   Anthony De Mello, *The Way to Love: The Last Meditations of Anthony de Mello* (New York: Image, 1995).

7.   Lion's Roar Staff, "What is the Meaning of the Lotus in Buddhism?" *Lion's Roar*, January 17, 2018, https://www.lionsroar.com/what-is-the-lotus/.

8.   Bhikkhu Bodhi, *The Numerical Discourses of the Buddha* (Somerville, MA: Wisdom Publications, 2012), 4.36.

9. Wayne Teasdale, *The Mystic Heart: Discovering a Universal Spirituality in the World's Religions* (Novato, CA: New World Library, 2001).

10. The Dalai Lama quotes this third-century BCE inscription in his book *Beyond Religion: Ethics for a Whole World* (Boston: Houghton Mifflin Harcourt, 2011).

11. John R. Mabry, *A Christian Walks in the Footsteps of the Buddha* (Berkley, CA: The Apocryphile Press, 2014), 12.

12. Gandhi in *Young India* (December 22, 1927), https://www.gandhiashramsevagram.org/what-jesus-means-to-me/sermon-on-the-mount.php.

13. Stanley Rowland, Jr., "2,500 Here Hail Boycott Leader," *New York Times* (March 26, 1956).

14. Quoted by David Steindl-Rast in *Gethsemani Encounter: A Dialogue on the Spiritual Life by Buddhist and Christian Monastics,* Donald Mitchell and James Wiseman, eds. (New York: Bloomsbury, 1999), 274.

15. Richard Rohr, *The Universal Christ: How a Forgotten Reality Can Change Everything We See, Hope for, and Believe* (New York, Convergent, 2019), 210.

16. Eknath Easwaran, *Original Goodness: A Commentary on the Beatitude* (Petaluma, CA: Nilgiri Press, 1989), 24. This quote is often, mistakenly, attributed to Meister Eckhart.

17. Meg Llewellyn, *Celtic Miracles and Wonders: Tales of the Ancient Saints* (Vestal, NY: Anamchara Books, 2015), 27–29.

18. Ibid.

19. Thomas Cahill, *How the Irish Saved Civilization: The Untold Story of Ireland's Heroic Role from the Fall of Rome*

to the Rise of Medieval Europe (New York: Doubleday, 1995), 158.

20. Ibid.

21. Ibid., 159.

22. Gerald Mulligan, "Settling Down or Moving On? The Settlement of the Irish Neolithic Landscape," *New Hibernia Review 16* (1: 2012), 94–112.

23. John Steven, "What Is an Enso?" *Lion's Roar* (June 1, 2007), https://www.lionsroar.com/what-is-an-enso/.

Chapter 2: Celtic Spirituality and Hinduism

24. Ellyn Sanna, "Christ in Creatures," in *Celtic Nature Prayers*, Kenneth McIntosh and Lucie Stone, eds. (Vestal, NY: Anamchara Books, 2015), 44–45.

25. Bede Griffiths, *The Golden String* (London: The Harvill Press, 1954), 9.

26. Thomas Merton, *Conjectures of a Guilty Bystander* (New York: Image Books, 1965), 153.

27. Quoted in Peter Berresford's "Meet the Brahmins of Ancient Europe, the High Caste of Celtic Society," *Hindu Wisdom,* http://www.hinduwisdom.info/articles_hinduism/258.htm.

28. Ibid.

29. *Hinduism Today*, "The Celts" (March 1, 1994), https://www.hinduismtoday.com/magazine/may-1994/1994-05-the-celts/.

30. Fanny Feehan, "Suggested Links Between Eastern and Celtic Music," in *The Celtic Consciousness*, Robert O'Driscoll, ed. (New York: George Braziller, 1982), 334.

31. *Hinduism Today.*

32. David Frawley, "Nakshatras and Upanakshatras," American Institute of Vedic Studies (January 13, 2012), https://web.archive.org/web/20150322154946/https://vedanet.com/2012/06/13/nakshatras-and-upanakshatras/.

33. Berresford.

34. Ibid.

35. Doris Srinivasan, *Concept of Cow in the Rigveda* (Delhi: Motilal Banarsidass, 1979).

36. Devdutt Pattanaik, "Food Is Truth," *Scroll.in* (July 19, 2016), https://scroll.in/article/811994/.

37. John Leavitt, "The Cow of Plenty in Indo-Iranian and Celtic Myth," *Journal of Indo-European Studies 35* (2000), 210.

38. Amy Sherwood, "An Bó Bheannaithe: Cattle Symbolism in Traditional Irish Folklore, Myth, and Archaeology," *PSU McNair Scholars Online Journal* 3 (1: 2009), article 21, https://doi.org/10.15760/mcnair.2009.189 .

39. Brian Wright, *Brigid: Goddess, Druidess and Saint* (Stroud, UK: The History Press, 2011).

40. Steve Gagnon, "How Much of an Atom Is Empty Space?" *Questions and Answers*, https://education.jlab.org/qa/how-much-of-an-atom-is-empty-space.html.

41. Robert Kolb, Irene Dingel, and Ľubomír Batka, eds., *The Oxford Handbook of Martin Luther's Theology* (Oxford, UK: Oxford University Press, 2014), 97, 197.

42. Alexander Carmichael, *Carmina Gadelica* (Edinburgh, UK: Floris Books, 1992), 199.

43. Columbanus in *Celtic Spirituality*, Oliver Davies, ed. (Mahwah, NJ: Paulist Press, 2007), Sermon Five.

44. Cynthia Bourgeault, *The Wisdom Jesus: Transforming Heart and Mind—A New Perspective on Christ and His Message* (Boulder, CO: Shambhala, 2008), chapter 2.

45. Meg Llewellyn, *Celtic Miracles and Wonders: Tales of the Ancient Saints* (Vestal, NY: Anamchara Books, 2015), 22, 37.

46. George McLeod, quoted in *George MacLeod: Founder of the Iona Community* (Iona, UK: Wild Goose Publications, 2001), 426.

47. Mark Twain, *Following the Equator* (New York: American Publishing Company, 1897), 187.

48. In 2021, the Pew Research Center reported that 61 percent of Hindus in India believe in "only one God with many manifestations." Seven percent believe "there are many gods." Neha Sahgal, Jonathan Evans, Ariana Monique Salazar, et al., "Religion in India: #12. Beliefs About God," Pew Research Center (June 29, 2021), https://www.pewresearch.org/religion/2021/06/29/beliefs-about-god-in-india/.

49. Eknath Easwaran, trans., *The Upanishads* (Tomale, CA: Nilgiri Press, 2007), 169.

50. "Song of Amergin," in *Lebor Gabála Érenn: The Book of Invasions,* §65–95, online from the Celtic Literature Collective, http://www.maryjones.us/ctexts/lebor5.html.

51. Sahgai, et al. According to Pew's research, 69 percent of Indian Hindus believe God can be manifested in Nature, such as mountains, rivers and trees, and 62 percent say God can be manifested in animals; the same share say God can appear through human beings. Also according

to Pew's research, Hindus are much more likely than those in other religious communities to believe that each of these manifestations is possible.

52. Eknath Easwaran, *Essence of the Upanishads* (Tomales, CA: Nilgiri, 2009), II.2.2, 93.

53. Monier Monier-Williams, *A Sanskrit-English Dictionary* (Oxford, UK: Oxford University Press, 1923), 90.

54. Pavulraj Michael, "'Avatar' and Incarnation: Gita Spirituality and Ignatian Spirituality at the Crossroads," *Gregorianum 97* (2: 2016), 323–342.

55. Karl Rahner, "On the Theology of the Incarnation," in *Theological Investigations Volume 4* (Abingdon, UK: Helicon Press, 1961), 117–118.

56. Nick Sutton, *Introduction to Hindu Texts, History, and Philosophy* (Oxford, UK: Oxford Centre for Hindu Studies, 2023), 122.

57. Hindu American Foundation, "Oneness and Pluralism: Hinduism's Essence," https://www.hinduamerican.org/hinduism-basics (accessed February 20, 2023).

58. Kauai's Hindu Monastery, "Why Does Hinduism Have So Many Gods?" *Basics of Hinduism* (2023), https://www.himalayanacademy.com/readlearn/basics/.

59. Nancy Frackenberry, "Classical Theism, Panentheism, and Pantheism: On the Relation Between God Construction and Gender Construction," *Zygon 28* (1: 1993), 29–46.

60. In F. Max Muller, ed., *Rig-Veda-Sahita: The Sacred Hymns of the Brahmans Together with the Commentary of Sayanakarya,* Vol. IV (London: Henry Frowde, 1892), 10.90.3–4.

61. Robert Van Der Wyer, *Celtic Fire* (London: Darton, Longman, Todd, 1990), 96.

62. Deirdre Carabine, *John Scotus Eriugena* (New York: Oxford University Press, 2000), 33.

63. Sarvepalli Radhakrishnan, *Eastern Religions and Western Thought* (Oxford, UK: Oxford University Press, 1940), 20, 24, 294.

64. Karan Singh, "The Growing Relevance of Vedanta," *India International Centre Quarterly 40* (1: 2013), 18.

65. Swami Sarvapriyananda, "The Four Yogas," (Hollywood, CA: The Vendanta Society of Southern California), available online at https://home.csulb.edu/~wweinste/yogas.html.

66. John of the Cross, *The Ascent of Mount Carmel,* quoted in Huston Smith's *The World's Religions* (New York: Harper Collins, 2009), 28.

67. John Scotus Eriugena, *Periphyseon on the Division of Nature*, I.P. Sheldon-Williams, trans. (Washington, DC: Dumbarton-Oaks, 1987), 390.

68. *Bhagavad Gita* (Tomales, CA: Nilgiri, 2007), 89.

69. John Carey, *King of Mysteries: Early Irish Religious Writings* (Dublin: Colour Books Limited, 2000), 77.

70. Natalie Y. Moore, "In Hindu Worship, Music Is Gift to Gods," *Chicago Tribune* (May 12, 2006), https://www.chicagotribune.com/.

71. Syama Allard, "The Power of Music, According to Hinduism," *Hindu American Foundation* (October 1, 2021), https://www.hinduamerican.org/.

72. Alexander Carmichael, *Carmina Gadelica Vol. 1* (Edinburgh, UK: T. and A. Constable, 1900), 5.

73. V. Jayaram, "The Ten Amazing Benefits of Pilgrimages in Hinduism" (2019), https://www.hinduwebsite.com/.

74. Baba Hari Dass, ed., *Srimad Bhagavad Gita: Volume 2* (Santa Cruz, CA: Sri Rama, 2013), 27.

75. Story told in John Templeton's *Agape Love: Tradition in Eight World Religions* (Philadelphia, PA: Templeton Foundation, 1999), 50.

76. This prayer, the only recorded writing of Brigid, was originally discovered in an ancient Gaelic manuscript in the Burgundian Library of Brussels.

77. *Bhagavad Gita*, 78.

78. In Ellyn Sanna's *Brother Lawrence: A Christian Zen Master* (Vestal, NY: Anamchara Books, 2011), 49.

79. Monier Williams, *Sanskrit English Dictionary with Etymology* (New York, Oxford University Press, 1998), 1201

80. Ibid.

81. Columba Marmion, *Christ the Ideal of the Monk* (Brewster, MA: Paraclete, 2014).

82. David E. Falk, "The Ark of the Covenant in its Egyptian Context," *Bible History Daily*, January 23, 2022, https://www.biblicalarchaeology.org/daily/biblical-artifacts/artifacts-and-the-bible/ark-of-the-covenant-in-egyptian-context/.

83. Michael Heiser, "Slaying the Sea Monster," *Bible Study Magazine*, July 27, 2017, https://www.biblestudymagazine.com/bible-study-magazine-blog/2017/7/20/slaying-the-sea-monster.

84. Quoted in Richard Geldard's *Remembering Heraclitus* (Great Barrington, MA: Lindisfarne Books, 2000), 156.

85. Anthony De Mello, *Sadhana, A Way to God: Christian Exercises in Eastern Form* (New York: Doubleday, 1978), 57.

86. Ibid., 39.

Chapter 3: Celtic Spirituality and Buddhism

87. Jack Kornfield in Marcus Borg's *Jesus and Buddha: The Parallel Sayings* (Berkeley, CA: Ulysses Press, 2023), 8.

88. Fedir Androshchuk, "Rural Vikings and Viking Helgo," in *Cultural Interactions Between East and West. Archaeology, Artefacts and Human Contacts in Northern Europe* (Stockholm: Stockholm Studies in Archaeology, 2007), 153–163.

89. Laurence Cox, *Buddhism and Ireland: From the Celts to the Counter-Culture and Beyond* (Sheffield, UK: Equinox, 2013).

90. M. Scott Peck, *The Road Less Traveled, Timeless Edition: A New Psychology of Love, Traditional Values and Spiritual Growth* (New York: Touchstone, 2003), 15.

91. Pelagius, *On the Christian Life*, in Oliver Davies, *Celtic Spirituality* (Mahwah, NJ: Paulist Press, 1999), 402.

92. John Cassian, *Conferences*, Colm Luibheid, trans. (Mahwah, NJ: Paulist Press, 1985), 11.

93. Dorotheus of Gaza, *Discourses and Sayings,* Eric Wheeler, trans. (Collegeville, MN: Liturgical Press, 1977), 89.

94. Anthony De Mello, *The Way to Love*, 20.

95. Ibid., 24–25.

96. Nyogen Senzaki, *101 Zen Stories* (New York: David McKay, 1940), 18.

97. Jack Maguire, *Essential Buddhism: A Complete Guide to Beliefs and Practices* (New York: Pocket Books, 2001), 90–91.

98. Community of Aidan and Hilda USA, "Our Way of Life," https://aidanandhilda.wordpress.com/our-way-of-life/. (Italics are mine.)

99. Thich Nhat Hanh, *Living Buddha, Living Christ* (New York: Riverhead Books, 1995), 56. (Italics are in the original.)

100. Maguire, 118.

101. Melody D. Knowles, "A Woman at Prayer: A Critical Note on Psalm 131," *Journal of Biblical Literature 125* (2: 2006), 385–389.

102. Peter Berresford Ellis, *A Brief History of the Celts* (London: Constable & Robinson, 2003), 101–102.

103. Carl McColman, *An Invitation to Celtic Wisdom: A Little Guide to Mystery, Spirit, and Compassion* (Charlottesville, VA: Hampton Roads, 2018), 45–46.

104. John Cassian, *Conferences*, Colm Luibhéid, trans. (Mahwah, NJ: Paulist Press, 1985), 15

105. Ibid., 101.

106. For directions on how to do Centering Prayer, see Contemplative Outreach (founded by Father Keating): https://www.contemplativeoutreach.org/centering-prayer-method/.

107. Thich Nhat Hanh, *Living Buddha, Living Christ* (New York: Penguin, 2007), 76.

108. Solas Bhride Center and Hermitages, "Celebrating the Tenth Anniversary of the Visit of the Dalai Lama," (April 16, 2021), https://solasbhride.ie/celebrating-the-10th-anniversary-of-the-visit-of-the-dalai-lama/.

109. Ibid.

110. Tertullian, *The Writings of Tertullian* (Woodstock, ON: Devoted, 2017), 48.

111. Origen, *Contra Celsum* (Cambridge, UK: Cambridge University Press, 1980), 132.

112. Alan Kreider, "The Pacifism of the Early Church," in *A Matter of Faith: A Study Guide for Churches on the Nuclear Arms Race* (Washington, DC: Sojourners, 1981), 44.

113. Chad Gerber, "The Real Story Behind Constantine's Conversion," *Our Sunday Visitor* (October 17, 2012), https://www.osvnews.com/2012/10/17/the-real-story-behind-constantines-conversion/.

114. Hippolytus of Rome, *The Treatise on the Apostolic Tradition*, Gregory Dix, trans. (London: Routledge, 1937), 26.

115. Sulpitius Severus, *On the Life of St. Martin* (Putty, NSW: St. Shenouda Monastery, 2013). Severus, who wrote Martin's biography, was his contemporary and close friend.

116. Bhikshuni Thubten Chodron, "Sorrow and Hope: A Prayer to Kuan Yin" (April 2, 2018), https://thubtenchodron.org/.

117. Jack Kornfield, "Statement on Racism from Buddhist Teachers & Leaders in the United States" (May 15, 2015), https://jackkornfield.com/statement-on-racism-from-buddhist-teachers-leaders-in-the-united-states/.

Chapter 4: Celtic Spirituality and Taoism

118. George Lucas, *The Last Jedi* (Walt Disney Studios: 2017).

119. Brigid Emily Herman, *Creative Prayer* (New York:

Cosimo Classics, 2007), 28.

120. Qiguang Zhao, *Do Nothing & Do Everything: An Illustrated New Taoism* (St. Paul, MN: Paragon House, 2010), 20.

121. John R. Mabry*, God as Nature Sees God: A Christian Reading of the Tao Te Ching* (Berkeley, CA: Apocrophile Press, 1994), 1.

122. Lao Tzu, *Tao Te Ching: An Illustrated Journey*, Stephen Mitchell, trans. (London: Frances Lincoln, 1999), 25. All subsequent quotations from the Tao Te Ching are from this translation unless otherwise noted.

123. George Lucas, *The Empire Strikes Back* (20th Century Studios, 1980).

124. Robert Van Der Wyer, *Celtic Fire* (London: Darton, Longman, Todd, 1990), 96.

125. Ilia Delio, *A Hunger for Wholeness: Soul, Space, and Transcendence* (Mahwah, NJ: Paulist Press, 2018), 27.

126. Richard Rohr, *The Universal Christ* (New York: Convergent, 2021), 13.

127. Mabry, 5

128. Mabry, 1, 52.

129. Lynne Bundesen, *The Feminine Spirit at the Heart of the Bible* (Vestal, NY: Anamchara Books, 2019), 15–16. I highly recommend this book for all serious Bible readers. It is a scholarly yet accessible, extremely thorough journey through the Bible, from Genesis in the Hebrew scriptures to the Book of Revelation at the end of the Christian scriptures, revealing the Divine Feminine that has been present all along in scripture,.

130. Gilbert Markus, trans., *The Life of St Cainnech of Aghaboe*

(2018), available online at: https://uistsaints.co.uk/wp-content/uploads/2018/10/Vita-Sancti-Cainnechi-with-GM-translation-and-notes.pdf.

131. Patrick Weston Joyce, *A Social History of Ancient Ireland: Treating of the Government, Military System, and Law; Religion, Learning, and Art; Trades, Industries, and Commerce; Manners, Customs, and Domestic Life, of the Ancient Irish People, Volume 2* (Dublin, UK: Longman, Green & Co, 1913), 526.

132. Zhao, 53.

133. Zhao, 15.

134. Thomas Traherne, "Wonder," *The Broadview Anthology of Seventeenth-Century Verse and Prose,* Alan Rudrum, Holly Faith Nelson, and Joseph Black, eds. (Peterborough, ON: Broadview Press, 2000), 1087.

135. Carl Jung, "Mysterium Coniunctionis: An Inquiry into the Separation and Synthesis of Psychic Opposites in Alchemy," *The Collected Works of C. G. Jung, Volume 14,* R. F. C. Hull, trans. (Princeton, NJ: Princeton University Press, 1976), 419–420.

136. Rumi, paraphrased by Devon Holcombe in *Love Prayers from Rumi and Other Sufi Mystics* (Vestal, NY: Anamchara Books, 2018), 35.

137. Ray Simpson, *Pilgrim Way* (Rattlesden, UK: Kevin Mayhew, 2005), 177.

138. Ibid., 178

139. Alan Watts, *Behold the Spirit: A Study in the Necessity of Mystical Religion* (New York: Pantheon, 1949), 175.

140. Zhao, 31.

141. Zhao, 56.

INDEX

Discover more
books by
Kenneth McIntosh—

Water from an Ancient Well

Celtic Spirituality for Modern Life:
Pilgrimage Study Edition

This new version has more than 150 pages of previously unpublished material, including illustrated guides to Celtic pilgrimage sites, study questions, and updated research.

Using story, scripture, reflection, and prayer, Kenneth McIntosh offers us a taste of the living water that refreshed the ancient Celts, allowing them to perceive God as a living Presence in everybody and everything. This Earth-based and inclusive perspective suggests life-giving alternatives to modern faith practices, opening the door to a Christianity big enough to embrace the entire world.

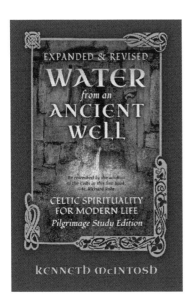

"If you want to run away to paradise for a couple of days, and drink living water from a source unlike any other, read Kenneth McIntosh's deeply satisfying book."

— Leonard Sweet,
best-selling author of
Nudge: Awakening Each Other to the God Who's Already There and *So Beautiful: Divine Design for Life and the Church*

Celtic Nature Prayers

Prayers from an Ancient Well

Find God in Nature

Pray for Our Endangered Planet

Long before they had heard about Christianity, the Celts knew that Nature was their portal to a great spiritual reality. Wells, mountain crags, caves, and lochs were "thin places" that allowed access to the realm of spirits. In these temples of Nature, the Celts sought physical and spiritual healing, as well as revelation. The salmon, the eagle, and even the tiny hazelnut, all were allies in helping humanity access the mysterious magic that underlay physical matter.

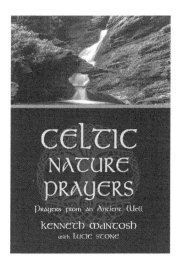

Reading the Bible the Celtic Way
The Peacock's Tail Feathers

Learn how the ancient Christian Celts read the Bible—
and discover new ways to understand
the sacred Scriptures today.

The Celts' perspectives on the Bible were far less literal than many modern viewpoints, and yet at the same time, they treasured even deeper layers of meaning than are familiar to most twenty-first century readers. For the Celts, Scripture was a wondrous treasure trove of metaphor and meaning, stories and symbols, all pointing to the loving Mystery that weaves through all Reality.

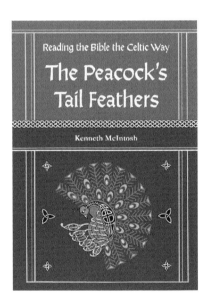

Hope in an Age of Fear
Wisdom from the Book of Revelation

The Book of Revelation has been misunderstood as a book of future predictions and escape from the world—but it is actually a survival and transformation guide, written for people whose lives were threatened by the first-century system of domination. Kenneth McIntosh goes through the entire book, chapter by chapter, revealing Revelation's abundance of wisdom we can apply to the challenges we face in today's world.

May these visions of transformation bring renewal to your inner self, giving hope for yourself and for the world that is struggling around you.

Brigid's Mantle

A Celtic Dialogue Between
Pagan and Christian

Long ago, the story goes, Brigid flung out her mantle over the world. Beneath its shelter, the Earth and its people could find healing, insight, and growth. This legend, shared by both Celtic Pagans and Celtic Christians, makes the point that a mantle is not a box, a small rigid container meant to keep some things inside while excluding others. Instead, a mantle is wide, flexible, inclusive. Using this as their central metaphor, the authors—one a Pagan healer and the

other a Christian minister—engage in a dialogue that is ultimately about what it means to be spiritual, to be a person of faith. While the authors affirm that very real differences separate Paganism and Christianity, they affirm that shared points of understanding can be found under "Brigid's Mantle."

Contemplative Coloring
The Green Man

More and more people are rediscovering what they already knew when they were kids—coloring is fun. What's more, coloring can lead us into a deeper awareness of both our inner selves and the world around us.

The Green Man images in this coloring book have been paired with short quotations from other writings by Kenneth McIntosh. These quotations are offered for use as mental focal points as you color, with space provided for you to jot down any thoughts that may rise to the surface.

Anamchara
Books

AnamcharaBooks.com

Made in the USA
Columbia, SC
17 October 2023